Spouse Calls

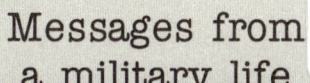

Messages from
a military life

W0082730

ROYAL

Terri Barnes

Elva Resa ✳ Saint Paul

Columns in this collection first appeared in *Stars and Stripes*.
Column dates varied by edition; the dates used in this book reflect
the earliest date the column appeared in print or online.

Cover design by Connie DeFlorin and Andermax Studios. Photos
courtesy of Terri Barnes, Minnesota National Guard, and Karen
Pavlicin-Fragnito.

Terri's lifelong dream to become an author began in junior high,
with her first story attempts pecked out at her grandmother's house
on the typewriter featured on the front cover.

Library of Congress Cataloging-in-Publication Data

Barnes, Terri, 1963-
  Spouse calls : messages from a military life / Terri Barnes.
      pages cm
  ISBN 978-1-934617-25-0 (pb) -- ISBN 978-1-934617-26-7 (epub
ebook) -- ISBN 978-1-934617-27-4 (kindle ebook)
1. Barnes, Terri, 1963- 2. Military spouses--United
States--Biography--Anecdotes. 3. United States--Armed Forces--
Military life--Anecdotes. I. Title.
  U766.B35 2014
  355.0092--dc23
  [B]
                        2013050186

Printed in United States of America.
10 9 8 7 6 5 4 3 2 1

Elva Resa Publishing
8362 Tamarack Vlg., Ste. 119-106, St. Paul, MN 55125

www.ElvaResa.com
www.MilitaryFamilyBooks.com
www.SpouseCalls.com

*This book is dedicated to
Mark, who is my very own military hero;
our children, Will, Jessie, and Wesley;
and Mom, who first showed me what being a military wife is all about.*

*In memory of my father, MSgt. Jimmie L. Hurley, USAF (Ret.)
1941-2009*

★

Contents

Introduction

I'm a military spouse, but I've never stood on a windy pier or tarmac dressed in red, white, and blue, holding a baby and waving an American flag. Variations on that image turn up unfailingly on television, online, or in print whenever the subject of military families arises. I often suspect a similar loop plays inside the heads of people I meet when they find out my husband serves in the military.

Yes, he's been deployed several times. Cue the surprise homecoming footage: Uniformed dad popping out of a giant gift-wrapped box. Haven't done that either. And I call myself a military wife?

Yes, I do.

These well-known scenes are dramatic, poignant, and real. They are parts of the military story, but not the whole. Pictures speak more than a thousand words, but a thousand words or even ten thousand couldn't convey the message of military life. Because there isn't just one message. There isn't just one story. There's one for every person who lives it.

My father served two tours in Southeast Asia. He spent more peaceful tours in many other places, retiring after twenty years on active duty. My husband has been deployed five times during three combat operations: Desert Storm, Enduring Freedom and Iraqi Freedom. My family has certainly been touched by war and affected by it, but we have been shaped more by the ordinary events of our lives as a military family.

Military life touches the consciousness of our nation mostly through events that are heroic, scandalous, or tragic. When combat claims military lives, when a general is caught in infidelity, or a former sailor commits horrific crimes, there's a concurrent spike in public interest. However, the quieter days, when no one is watching, are more indicative of our lives than big news events. Much of military life is noteworthy without being newsworthy.

I first began writing Spouse Calls for *Stars and Stripes* in 2007, when our nation was at war on two fronts. I wanted the column to include practical content, news, and helpful information for military families. But before long, smaller pieces of my life began to find their way into my work, from deployments and memorial services to packing lunches and baking cookies.

When I was trying to write a column, the daily events of my military life would stand at my elbow and whisper—or shout—that they were part of the message, too. I had no choice but to listen, and write.

I've encountered wounded warriors while walking the halls of Walter Reed and Landstuhl, but I've never been to either hospital looking for a news story. I was there for a mammogram, perhaps, or to take one of my children for an eye appointment. This is where military families live our lives, in the intersection of conflict and the commonplace. Perhaps that's the crux of military life, and the best place to find messages from the home front.

In this collection of Spouse Calls columns, I don't presume to tell the whole story of military life. I can only write about what I've seen, where I've been, whom I've met, contributing to the larger picture of military families, one that fleshes out the real people and real lives we live.

These are just a few of the messages from military life.

★ ★ ★

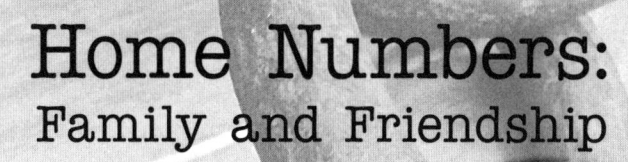

Home Numbers:
Family and Friendship

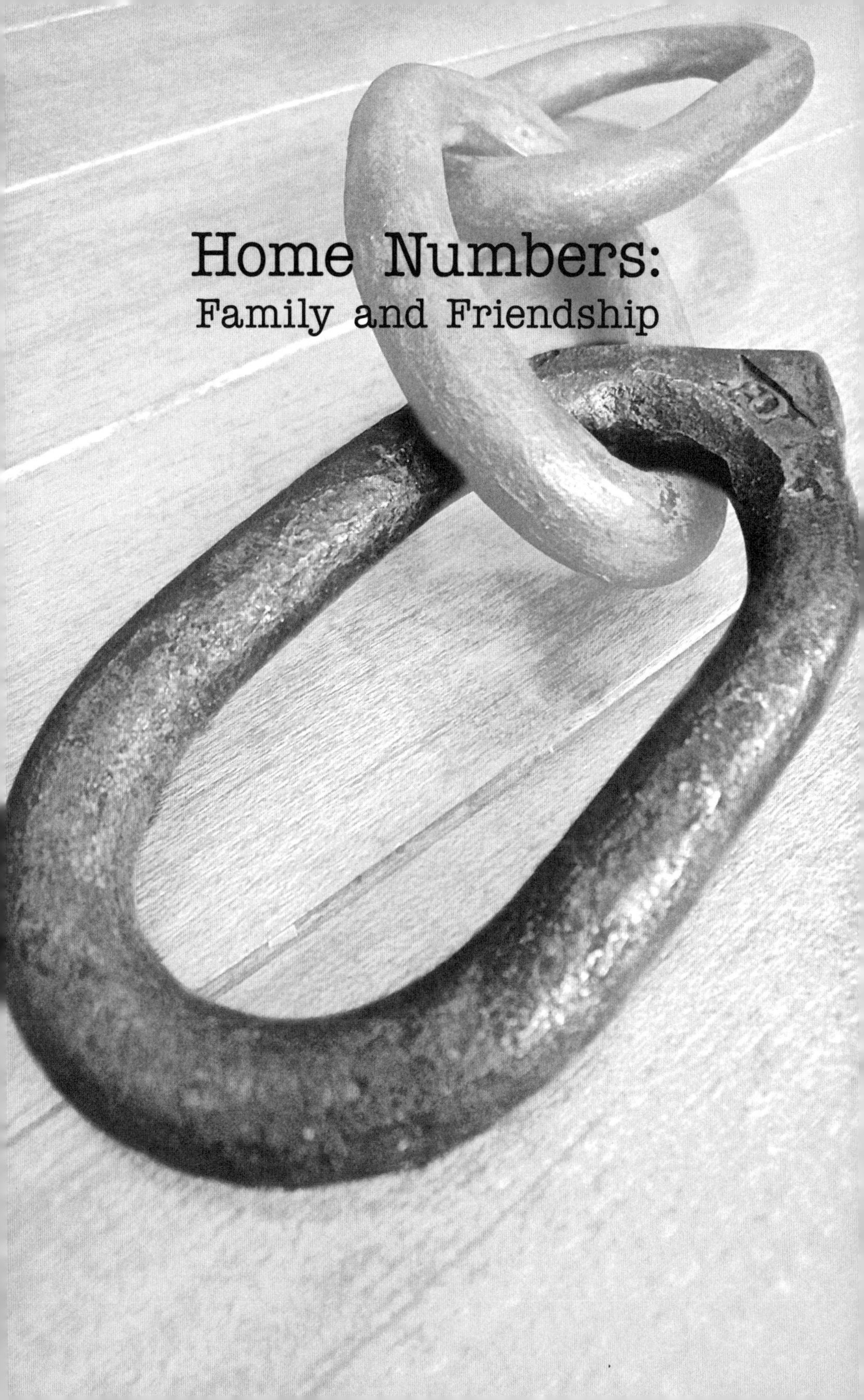

Dream Houses

February 8, 2013

Some people wait their entire lives to find their dream home. I've already lived in several.

At our first assignment in Texas, my husband and I lived in our first real house. It was my dream home because it had a fireplace. We didn't have much furniture to put in it. And we used a rotary push mower, a gift from my grandfather, until we could afford a gas-powered lawn mower to cut the grass. It had a big backyard, a rectangle of concrete for a patio, and even a grapevine.

Our first on-base home, at Sheppard Air Force Base, Texas, was my dream home because it had hardwood floors and big windows. We brought our first baby home there.

Our second baby came home to a dream house on a tropical island, complete with a hibiscus bush and a hammock between two palm trees. Our house on Andersen Air Force Base, Guam, wasn't much to look at. With concrete walls, flat roof, and brown plywood shutters, it was more like a bunker, but it survived five typhoons and an earthquake, and it was less than ten minutes from the beach.

Our house on Luke Air Force Base, Arizona, was the house of my dreams mostly because it was *available*. After spending five months on the housing list in a sparsely furnished apartment with two small children, I could easily love the outdated cabinets, tiny closets, and oddly-paneled ceiling. By the time we left that dream house, with baby number three, we were bursting at its three-bedroom seams.

So naturally, our next dream house in Japan was even smaller. It had a closet under the stairs and, although we could have used the storage space, it got better use as a secret hideout, playhouse, or pirate cave on rainy days. Outside our windows, we had cherry blossoms in the spring and fiery red maple leaves in the fall.

Our dream home in Valdosta, Georgia, was a family favorite. It had a fireplace, a second story, plenty of space inside, and nearby woods and ponds outside. Dad and the kids built a tree house and picked blackberries for Mom to bake homemade cobblers. Quiet streets and lots of open spaces provided our children room for adventure and scope for the imagination.

At Los Angeles Air Force Base, California, our dream home had a view of the ocean and Catalina Island on a clear day from one of the upstairs windows, if you stood in just the right spot. The daily walk to the elementary school was a flower-lined sidewalk with a full view of the Pacific. With beautiful weather almost every day, we enjoyed our back patio and pergola. No fireplace, no air conditioning, but we rarely needed either one.

Our dream home at Ramstein, Germany, had three floors, a spiral staircase, balcony, and did I mention, was in Germany? Dream location and the last of our dream homes to house all our children year-round, it was walking distance down cobblestone streets to favorite restaurants, bakeries, and coffee shops.

Of all of these dream homes, our home in Virginia has the most space, which we most enjoy when it's full of our family and friends.

I don't know how many more dream homes we'll have. Someday we hope to have one that is truly ours and will be ours for a long time. When choosing it, I don't know that I'll be looking for the "must haves" the HGTV hosts rave about, such as granite countertops, recessed lighting, or a rain shower.

My "must haves" are a kitchen in which to cook for family and friends. A dining room big enough to hold them all. A sidewalk that leads into town. A sofa by the fireplace would be nice, and plenty of shelves for the books we like to read. Wall space for pictures from all over. Bedrooms for the beds our children used to jump on and dream on. Maybe their children will jump and dream on them, too.

When it's time to look for that dream home, I'll be looking for glimpses of the dreams from every home we've ever lived in.

★ ★ ★

Mom's Love Letter

May 9, 2010

I could write a lot about my mother: Her phone calls and emails provide advice and encouragement on everything from missing my college-aged son, to middle-school research papers, to prom dress decisions. She was present at the birth of all three of our babies, even the one born in Guam.

For love, a mom can endure fifteen hours on a plane—one way, not including layovers, without complaint—to welcome a new grandbaby. But there are harder things for love to endure, as well we know.

When I was nine or ten, my mother wrote me a letter. I don't remember when she gave it to me. I just remember having it when I was a little girl. It was short, only a few sentences, telling me she loved me, was proud of me, and encouraging me to hold on to my faith.

For a long time, I kept the letter in a secret compartment in the bottom of an old jewelry box. As a child, I had a habit of creating a hideout under my bed or in a corner of the attic, depending on where we lived. The jewelry box, my favorite books, and a flashlight were usually among the treasures found there.

I would take the letter out occasionally and—with the aid of my flashlight—read it and even shed tears over it, especially when one of us was angry. I knew that whatever punishment was meted out, whatever words passed between us, Mom loved me. Her words on the page reminded me.

When I was in high school, my parents' divorce precipitated a move to another house. I've made about twenty moves in my life as a military child and wife, but none has been as painful as that one.

Hurt and angry, I refused to help pack up my life for a move I bitterly resented. The treasure box was neglected, perhaps left behind in the attic, perhaps thrown away.

The letter was gone and forgotten, and after the dissolution of my family, the certainty that Mom's decisions were made out of love for me was gone, too. Our relationship was changed, tread-marked by the long procession of circumstances that follow a divorce, like slow-moving cars follow a hearse.

Years went by before I knew exactly what I had lost.

In fact, I was the mother of three young children when, one day, I suddenly remembered the jewelry box and its hidden contents. With bitter clarity, I also realized when it was lost and how. I couldn't believe I had forgotten it for so long, and I wished then that I could read the letter again.

Now, I'm the mother of three teenagers. My mother has written me many letters in the years since that difficult chapter of my family's history. She tells me often that she loves me, in words, deeds, and transoceanic flights.

I gave up the letter for lost, but rediscovered the certainty of my mother's love for me. Our relationship has been restored—not instantly, nor easily—but still, miraculously.

Last year, I was looking through my old journals. Behind the very last page of the very oldest volume—my life as a thirteen-year-old—I found the letter, yellowed by years and creased from many readings. I don't know how it got there or how the old pink diary kept its secret for so long. But it did.

Like the assurance of my mother's love, the letter was not truly lost, only misplaced, waiting to be found, read, and believed again.

★ ★ ★

Peace Stories

January 24, 2010

"Have you asked your dad about his war experiences?" the woman asked me.

As the interviewer, I was supposed to be the one asking questions, but perhaps this was to be expected from my interviewee, a retired Marine and currently a writing teacher.

The answer was no, and even as she encouraged me to do so, I knew that I would not. Several years ago, my father gave me his trove of photos from Vietnam, so I had pictures, but few words.

When my father and my husband would start swapping stories from their common Air Force experiences, I would listen carefully, gleaning details. Mostly, they talked about aircraft they had flown in or worked on. Dad liked to recall the people he knew, chuckling about crusty generals or "this ol' E-8 I flew with."

About the war, he was silent, and I respected his silence.

The woman's question came back to me when I received the news just after Christmas that my father was gone. A car accident claimed his life on December 30, 2009.

My earliest memory is of the day my dad returned from Vietnam. I woke up in the backseat of our car and saw his big round "wheel hat" silhouetted against the sun. I couldn't see his face, but I remember his voice as he leaned in to pick me up. I was two years old, so as far back as I can remember, I knew my dad had been to war, but he never told war stories.

He told other stories. When I was in grade school, we lived in Alaska. When Daddy would come home, I would sit on his lap, breathe in the smell of his flight suit, eat the dessert he saved from his flight lunch, and hear about the places he had been and the people who had flown with him.

I have an old photo that reminds me of one of his stories. It shows my dad, who was a crew chief, standing in front of his plane on a snowy tarmac, circa 1969. Beside him is Santa

Claus, who hitched a ride to help deliver supplies in remote Arctic areas. That was the kind of story Dad preferred to tell.

In letters from his overseas tours, the only hardship he mentioned was missing us, usually reminding me to say my prayers and mind my mother.

Only when I was older did I learn that Dad's mission in Vietnam was a dangerous one, flying over enemy territory, that he had lost friends there, that he had bad dreams.

Long after the war, as I was growing up, our family experienced other kinds of turmoil, which we weathered together and apart. Fallout from his untold stories? Perhaps, in part.

But do I regret not asking those questions? I don't think so. My father preferred not to talk about some experiences, but I've seen how those events shaped him and his life. I knew the man, so in some way I do know the stories, even the ones he didn't tell.

The words that mattered were said. When I talked to him on Christmas Day—from Germany to Texas—our last words to each other were what they always were at the end of a phone call: "I love you."

For Veteran's Day in 2008, I wrote a magazine article about my dad and his reluctance to tell war stories and sent him a copy. Now I'm especially glad that I did.

The closing lines were:

"Peace is not free or easy. It is hard won. It must be pursued and war stories are the story of that pursuit ... Still, the best stories are peace stories. Not fairy tales pretending that war and death and suffering don't happen, but true stories of peace reaching beyond conflict ... So thanks, Dad, for the peace stories. We owe our gratitude to you, and to all veterans who have endured the real story of war, so that others are free to hear the story of peace."

★ ★ ★

Worth More Than a Thousand Words
May 1, 2012

When my father died, he didn't leave me a fortune. He left me something better: his memories, even the ones he never talked much about. A few years before he died in 2009, he gave me a metal box filled with photos and home movies from my childhood. He handed it over when we were visiting him in Oklahoma, just as we were leaving. He said something offhand like, "The mice are getting to this stuff out in the barn. You should take it home with you."

Inside were boxes of photos and reels of 8mm film, taken when we were stationed in Texas, Colorado, and Alaska. Among the Polaroids and color slides from family vacations, I discovered something else.

A yellowed envelope labeled in Vietnamese and French enclosed two stacks of small black and white photos. The mice had found several, but most were intact.

I recognized my dad's handwriting on the backs of some. He had written brief descriptions like, "Unloading AC-123 at Quin Hon," or "Taking off at Bong Song." Some are aerial photos showing huts, mountains, airfields. I'm sure my father was the photographer. One says, "A train derailed—The V.C. tore the track out," and another, "Sailboats off the end of the runway Quin Hon." Many more photos were wordless, but they still told portions of the story of my dad as an airman in Vietnam in 1964 and 1965.

Some were from a trip to Saigon: a young boy giving my dad and his camera a mischievous wink and salute, a smiling woman carrying two big baskets on a shoulder pole, a man smoking a cigarette under the striped awning of the Saigon USO.

Others depict austere living conditions on base, looking all the more grim in monochromatic prints. Tents, hammocks, sandbags, guard towers. Makeshift runways made of Marston mats, expanses of modular corrugated steel.

My husband can identify most of the aircraft for me. It's the people who remain mysterious. Some snapshots show Dad's fellow airmen, friends perhaps.

A young captain reclines under the wing of a plane, wearing aviator sunglasses and a belt stocked with bullets. A paunchy sergeant stands on the runway, arms akimbo, the brim of his uniform cap flipped up. Two men repair landing gear. Another poses inside a bunker with helmet and weapon.

My father is in just a few photos. In one, he stands beside his plane at Bien Hoa Air Base, a pistol on his hip. On the nose of the plane is stenciled "Miss Terri Jane," my name and my mom's.

Mom has told me that Dad was a crewmember for a psychological warfare aircraft. Fitted with large speakers and no weapons, the small plane flew missions low over known enemy territory, blasting anticommunist messages and showering the ground with leaflets.

In another photo, a South Vietnamese soldier poses by the plane's loudspeakers. His name is not on the photo. I wonder if he flew with my dad and what happened to him. I wonder if my dad ever wondered the same thing.

I'll never know because I didn't ask him. Vietnam was a subject he rarely broached. I used to be satisfied with his silence. Now, there are questions I wish I could ask.

I have other photos, letters, and news clippings my mom and grandmother saved, mostly things my dad mailed home during the war. My mom collected her memories in a blue scrapbook, tied with a gold cord.

One news clipping was particularly enlightening. PFC Mike Mealey, reporting for the *Pacific Stars and Stripes* in December 1964, wrote about the missions and the dangers faced by the crews of propaganda planes like my dad's. Mealey's story said three such aircraft were in operation in Vietnam at the time.

That same month, Dad had sent home a Christmas card bearing the logo of the 21st Infantry Division Advisory Team. He was then at Can Tho, near the Mekong Delta, and mentioned the pilot quoted in the *Stripes* story.

"Dearest Darlings ... Capt. Scott and I were working with this outfit and they gave me this card ... You don't know how much I hate not having Xmas with my little family. But war is bad for a lot of people. I will try to write a letter tomorrow. Lot of love..."

Also in the scrapbook were newspaper stories of a tragic series of accidental explosions at Bien Hoa Air Base on May 16, 1965. Twenty-seven died and almost a hundred more were injured. Dad was there. My mom said she heard about it on the news, and it was two weeks before a cassette tape arrived from Dad.

"'First of all, I'm fine,' were his first words on the recording," she said.

"I was going out of my mind," she remembered. "We got news back then, but it wasn't as explicit as it is now."

I found a video of the aftermath of the Bien Hoa tragedy that someone posted on YouTube. I watched the men moving planes and fighting the fires, scanning every face for a glimpse of my dad. I knew those men had likely known him. I also knew that he had surely known some who died.

Dad would be seventy-one years old this month. The longer he is gone, the more conversations I wish we'd had. At least I have the pictures he took with his little black and silver camera.

When I was a teenager, the camera was lost somehow. Even years afterward, he would lament, "I sure wish I knew what happened to that camera." I used to wonder why it concerned him so much. Now I think I understand. It was his witness, and the pictures were his evidence. Now they're mine.

Each photo is a testimony, a piece of my dad's war story—the places he served, the men who served with him, scenes he thought were important enough to preserve when he was far from home.

Nothing in his bank account could make me richer.

~

This could have almost been my story. I, too, am a military spouse. My husband has proudly served the Army for twenty-one years now.

On May 1, I lit a candle in remembrance of my father, who left this world four years ago. When he fell ill, I had the privilege of tending to him. He was a proud man. I know it was the hardest thing he had probably done, but it was the least I could do for him. Every morning, I would drive over to the hospital to shave him and have breakfast together. It soon became my favorite time with him. He shared many stories over a cup of oatmeal, some from my early childhood years, and others of his military career as a medic.

What a proud soldier he was. He also served in Vietnam and Korea. Shortly before he passed, he handed me a box. In it were six reels of 8mm [film]. Memories of me and my brother growing up. [Dad] knew I had been longing for them.

Among his belongings, we also found a metal lockbox full of slides and tattered photos of his days serving his country abroad, his draft card, dog tags, and so much more. What peace it brought us when we looked through these precious items. We laughed some and cried some, but it gave us a glimpse of the father we really never knew.

We transferred to Germany a month after he passed ... Just a few months after arriving in Germany, my husband's unit was tasked with flag duty for the closing ceremonies of the Army base in Wurzburg. How ironic, as this was where my father was stationed in the '70s, the place where I had so many childhood memories of running around, carefree and happy.

As I watched the American and German flags slowly shimmy down the flagpole, I couldn't help but think of my dad. I wish I could turn back the hands of time and sit beside him just one more time as he told his stories. I wish I could ask him about the pictures we found. Sadly, that will never be.

Thank you for sharing your story and reminding me so much of my own father. I hope you will enjoy mine as well. Funny how similar life can be. —Angela B.

~

What a wonderful article!!! My dad was killed in Vietnam in 1970. How I wish I had just one letter. —*June Herring*

~

I am blessed to still have my father with us. He is eighty-eight years old and served in the Army at the end of WWII. Although I have seen some old photos and movies of his short military career, I realize there are probably more stories I haven't heard. On my next trip to Colorado to visit him, I'm going to sit down and ask him to share more of his past with me. I realize I won't have him around much longer. Thanks, Terri, for sharing this story about your dad. It prompted me to learn more about mine. —*Jan Richardson*

~

My brother and I lost our healthy, active dad far too suddenly in 2007. He was an Army helicopter pilot in Vietnam, and while I treasure the photographs and documents from his military service, there are so many questions I'd love to ask him.

My brother followed his footsteps and is currently serving in Afghanistan as a Kiowa helicopter pilot. It kills me that Dad isn't here to talk to him. He'd understand what my brother is going through far more deeply than my mother or I ever could. But we were so lucky to have him, and we're still following his lead. —*Laura F.*

★　★　★

No Strangers on This Train

February 21, 2010

Each of us has a story we like to tell, one that sums up our military spouse experience. It may be long and arduous, like a cross-country car trip with three kids, a dog, a cat, and no air conditioner. Or it may be brief and poignant, capturing a powerful moment like a snapshot.

Skippy's story is a little of both. Her name is Minnie, but a childhood moniker bestowed by her brother endured. Even Bill, whom she married in 1937, called her Skippy.

Being a military wife was not Skippy's whole life, but it was a significant chapter. Like many women of her era, she did her part in the early 1940s when Bill joined the Navy.

He served during World War II, at a time when the level of benefits and privileges military families enjoy today—for medical, housing, and travel needs—were unimaginable.

A machinist's mate aboard the USS Kennison, Bill's homeport was San Diego. Thousands of ships crowded the port during those war years, and with them hundreds of thousands of servicemen and families.

Unable to find a home in San Diego, the couple decided Skippy and their children would remain near family in Oklahoma and visit Bill when he was in port. When Skippy brought their toddler daughter and baby boy to visit Bill in California, they shared temporary housing with other sailors and their families.

The trip from Oklahoma took three days by train. Skippy made the sojourn on her own, carrying Tommy in his baby basket and holding Jane by the hand.

They often shared the ride with uniformed servicemen bound for ships that would take them to duty in the Pacific. Sometimes, friendly soldiers and sailors would buy Jane a bottle of Coca-Cola or play games with her, passing the time on the long journey, perhaps thinking of their own children or little sisters back home.

Following routes heavily traveled by servicemen during wartime also had hazards.

On one trip, when Skippy and her little brood arrived at the train station in Oklahoma City, a conductor stopped them, warning that only servicemen and their families were allowed to travel on the train.

"But my husband is in the Navy," she told him. "We're going to San Diego to meet him."

"Sorry," was the curt answer. "This train is for military only. If your husband isn't with you, you can't get on this train," and he turned away.

Skippy wondered how she and her children would be able to get to California to see Bill. A soldier, noticing her distress, approached her.

"Do you need some help?" he asked.

Holding back tears, she explained briefly, concluding, "My husband isn't with me, but I'm a sailor's wife."

"Well, you can be a soldier's wife today," he said. He offered her one arm, and took Tommy's basket in the other. Skippy held Jane's hand, and they got on the train unchallenged—a family in spirit, if not in fact. The soldier helped them find seats, and Skippy thanked him.

"I hope someone would do the same for my wife," he said, and disappeared in a crowd of khaki uniforms. She never saw him again.

Many years have passed, but she remembers.

Bill is gone now and greatly missed by Skippy, their four children, and eleven grandchildren. Great-grandchildren number more than twenty and counting.

Skippy celebrated her ninetieth birthday this week with family and friends in Oklahoma. I traveled from Germany to join them, because Bill and Skippy's little Jane grew up to be my mother.

While I'm here, I think I'll ask Meemaw to tell her story again. I never get tired of it.

★ ★ ★

The Family Forge

July 11, 2010

In a blacksmith shop he built himself, on land that once belonged to his parents, and on an anvil inherited from his grandfather, my uncle forges a chain. He takes a rod, pliable and glowing hot from the forge, and bends it into a loop. He sprinkles borax on the hot metal and explains that it will create a weld where the ends of the rod cross and join to become the first link of a chain.

"Better move back," he warns my children and me before sealing the weld with his hammer. Pounding the borax creates a shower of molten sparks. We "ooh" and "aah" like spectators at a fireworks display. I snap pictures like the tourist I am, even among my own kin.

He repeats the process, forging the links together, three in all, imprinting each with his own mark—a small anvil shape and his initials—and gives them to us. My aunt brings a pitcher of iced tea from the house, and we sit outside under the trees, enjoying the shade and a cool drink on a hot July day.

On another family visit, we take my grandmother out to lunch. There is a café in the small town near her house, the town where my parents and their brothers and sisters attended school and where many of their friends and families still live.

The bell over the door announces our arrival. A girl and a boy run toward us. "Meemaw!" they cry, throwing their arms around my grandmother. Though I haven't seen them since they were babies, their faces—full of family resemblance—are immediately familiar to me.

I say hello, and they smile shyly, clinging to Meemaw's legs. "This is your Aunt Terri," she says, patting each on the back. They are my cousin's children, but "aunt" seems more appropriate to our age difference.

Their mother is behind the counter. She says, "Hi, Meemaw," and to us, "We haven't seen y'all in a while." We get that a lot.

She is busy with a customer, but the kids sit down and have burgers and fries with us, taking up with our three children like old friends. How old will they be before we see them again?

On the drive home, I remember my young cousins' enthusiastic and affectionate greetings to my grandmother. My children love their Meemaw, but that kind of familiarity requires constant tending and visits much more frequent than once a year or so.

In our mobile military life, even visits to our families are nomadic. During vacation time or between assignments, we travel from place to place to visit our parents and siblings, forging the links of our extended family across eight states in two weeks' time. There is never enough time to see everyone—not enough to create the closeness I see between my more stationary relatives. But, it is enough to remind us we are part of something larger than our family of five.

Our links to our families are stretched by our travels around the world and back, but they are still strong. They remind us that when we are on the other side of the world, there are people who love us, pray for us, and think about us.

Those links assure us we are not alone, that there are people out there who have my grandfather's nose and my mother's eyes and a familiar last name. There are people who remember the day I was born and the day I got married, the day I embarked on this journey.

The chain my uncle made hangs in my house, a reminder that those links are there, even when we are far away from the family forge.

★ ★ ★

The Last Lunch

June 14, 2009

One night, a couple of weeks before the end of school, my oldest son said, "Hey, mom, this is the last time you'll have to pack three lunches." He said it like he was relieving me of a burden instead of breaking my heart.

Before you say it, yes, I know that all three of my children are perfectly capable of packing their own lunches, especially this one who is about to graduate from high school.

I pack their brown bags for myself as much as for them. It's something tangible to hand them as they head for the bus each morning. Whether they leave disgruntled or upbeat, I give them a kiss and a lunch. Whether they toss it in the first trash can they see, or eat and enjoy it, is really up to them once they walk out the door.

I have known since he started kindergarten what year my son would graduate from high school. I am perfectly aware that he is grown up, old enough to drive, to vote, to make his own decisions. All year, we've been marking high school "lasts": last homecoming, last home meet, last European Championships and—blessedly—his last time to take the SAT. The time is coming for him to be on his own, at least as far as college fits that description.

Somehow, though—blame it on the fact that seniors finish regular classes before the other students, or on latent denial—that last lunch thing sneaked up on me. With motherly sentimentality, along with his last sandwich, I included a silly note written on a leftover graduation party napkin.

His graduation party was typical for students at his Department of Defense school: a combined moving season farewell and celebration of high school's completion. We had it a few weeks before commencement to beat the wave of departures springtime always brings.

We cohosted the party with families of two of our son's close friends and fellow graduates. The festivities were at our house by default, because we're the only ones still in possession of real furniture, a grill, and kitchen utensils. Our movers come next month.

We had a house full of seniors, friends, and family, munching, talking, laughing, looking at old photos, and taking new ones.

Say what you will about transient military life, but it takes some kids a dozen or more years to make enough friends to fill a living room and spill into the backyard to celebrate their graduation. Military kids do it in three, two—or even one. They don't waste precious time.

At commencement, the principal recognized students who have attended our particular DoD school district since kindergarten. A collective murmur of "Wow" went up as six out of a couple hundred graduates stood up to resounding applause.

The irony of that moment hit me later. This is our world, where growing up and graduating in the same place is a novelty. Those six graduates must be as adept at making new friends as the waves of kids who flow in and out.

That skill and adaptability will serve them all well as they head into a new life.

Moving a continent away from home and family to go to college will be a challenge for our son and other military kids like him. It is somewhat familiar territory, though. He knows it can be done because he has seen it happen many times over.

He is equipped for adapting to a new environment and making new friends—this time on his own.

Like his last lunch, the bag of his experience as a military kid is packed. He can carry it with him wherever he goes. We'll hand it to him when he leaves. Whether he benefits from it is really up to him once he walks out the door.

I just hope he reads the note.

★ ★ ★

College Culture Shock

August 1, 2010

A brand new school year is in sight, and after a lifetime of living and moving with the family, some military kids are preparing to make their first solo transition—to college.

For those who have grown up in a military environment, particularly those who have spent a few years overseas, going to college in the US involves a modicum of culture shock.

Will, our first to leave the nest, graduated from a DoD high school in Germany. After his first year in college, I wanted to know his perspective on adjusting to life on "the outside."

What is it like to brave the civilian world on your own? How do fellow students react to your background? Here's what Will had to say to military kids bound for adventures in the civilian world.

~

As a military kid, explaining to someone outside the military where you are from is always a challenge. Do I tell them where I was born—a place I don't even remember—or where I've lived the longest, or where we go to visit my grandparents?

A simple question can turn into a lengthy discussion, whether you want it to or not. Now take this experience and multiply it by a few hundred, and you have your first few months as a freshman in college. Throw in a couple of overseas assignments, and you're in for even more explaining.

Although this seems like a bit of an inconvenience, it can definitely lead to some interesting conversations. Most cannot fathom that you went to two or maybe even three high schools or that you lived in Germany for three years and don't speak German. The latter can be a little embarrassing.

Some people, when they find out you are "from" another country, will say crazy things, like "Wow, your English is really good." They just can't comprehend the way we have grown up.

The fact is, as a military brat, you've had a radically different childhood than most, and often you bring more to the table.

You didn't just read about D-Day in a textbook, you've walked on the beaches of Normandy. You've seen the Mona Lisa, the Rosetta Stone—the real hardware, not the software version—Mt. Fuji, and countless other artifacts and locations that are integral to the history of our world.

As a military child, you may not have gotten your driver's license at sixteen, or lived in the same town as your grandparents, or gone to the same high school that your mom did. Often, you might feel as if you've missed out because you didn't have these experiences. Often, it is a challenge to relate to those who don't understand the military life.

However, because you are different, people are curious. They want to share your experiences and get to know you—someone who hasn't lived in the same town his whole life.

After all, college is a chance to engage in a new life, to start fresh and meet new and different people. Especially for those who have been in an exclusively-military community, it is important to realize that these people, with whom you now live, may not fully understand your way of life, but accept you all the same.

In many ways, as a college freshman, you are in the same boat as all your classmates. Each is embarking on a journey through unfamiliar waters. Even though you might be going back to a home you've never lived in when the semester ends, you are not as different as you might think.

★ ★ ★

Strings Attached

May 3, 2011

"You've got to cut the cord, Mom."

This piece of sage advice brought to you by my twenty-year-old son. It's his way of comforting me (from Texas) as I'm preparing to send his younger sister off to college (in California). Did I mention our family is moving this summer (to Virginia)? What part of "nearest and dearest" do these kids not understand? The "nearest" part, apparently.

I've always been proud of my children's willingness to pick up and go, to consider any new military assignment as their home, to adapt to almost any situation. However, I've discovered there is a limit to my admiration for their no-strings attitude. It's at the end of the string that ties them to me. Probably the one my son thinks I need to cut.

"Now you know how I feel."

This slice of cold comfort brought to you by my mother. It's her way of sympathizing with me (from Oklahoma) while I'm (in Germany) bemoaning the distance that will separate me from my two oldest children next year.

Okay, so she is right. I have no one to blame but myself—well, possibly my military husband. When our children were toddlers, who scarcely noticed when they moved, we encouraged them to become grade-schoolers who viewed each move as an adventure. When they were young teens who left friends tearfully, we taught them to believe they could make friends anywhere. Now they are young adults who embrace their global upbringing to the extent that living on the same planet with their parents seems close enough.

Children who have watched us live for years far away from our own parents may assume that far away is the natural place for parents.

"But that's not what I meant!"

This attempt at backpedaling brought to you by me. This is my way of coping with a consequence of our nomadic life that I did not foresee—if you consider denial a means of coping. I wonder now how I could have missed such an obvious natural progression. Children who have been taught that home can be anywhere have the confidence to believe they can make anywhere their home—without respect to parental proximity.

Someone will no doubt wish to point out that the goal of parenting is to work oneself out of a job, that raising children to stay home is pointless. So before you write that letter, let me just say, "You're right—but not helpful." What I want right now is sympathy, tissues, and frequent flyer miles, not platitudes.

Maybe in a few years, I'll be adjusted to looser family ties. Then I'll be able to throw around pithy phrases about empty nests with the best of them.

But to tell the truth, I don't like the thought of that future me with calluses on her heart where the strings once were. I'd rather think that the strings would stay attached but become more elastic, connecting without binding, perhaps encouraging my children to draw closer again.

I'm not asking for the same zip code, although that would be nice. I am hoping for the same time zone, but if I've learned anything in a lifetime of military moving, it is that feeling close to those you love has little to do with geography or Greenwich Mean Time.

My mother assures me this process is painful for all parents, military and otherwise. She said it helps to know your children are prepared to choose and travel their own path.

"You will always miss your children," Mom told me. "But it's a different kind of missing when you know they are where they need to be."

Wise ones advise us to give our children roots and wings. In our mobile life, I wonder if we've given them too much of one and not enough of the other. We're in the process of launching our children out of the nest while our nest is in motion. What kind of crazy life is this?

The only one we know—the one we've taught our children to love. This foregone conclusion brought to you by me.

★ ★ ★

I Am Somebody

June 7, 2011

It's that "Pomp and Circumstance" time of year. The recurrent ritual of caps, gowns, and tassels touches our household tomorrow as our daughter, Jessie, graduates from high school.

In a class assignment, she wrote about moving around as a military child and how it shaped her life and personality. I asked Jessie if I could share some of her words here.

~

No one in Los Angeles wanted to be friends with the pale, frizzy-haired short girl. So for the longest time, I held my place well as a "nobody." After moving a few times and finding who I was, I discovered that being "nobody" at one school doesn't mean you are nobody at all. I have moved seven times in my life so far, and I plan to make my eighth move this summer as I venture out into the real world.

I was born in Guam, a freckle on the wide face of the South Pacific Ocean. We flew to Luke Air Force Base in Arizona about a year afterward. Four years and a baby brother later, I moved to Yokota Air Base in Japan—still among my favorite places to live.

After first grade, our family returned to the States. We lived in Alabama for a year. Moody AFB in Georgia was next on the list. There, we had porch swings, tree houses, a yard big enough to play baseball, blackberry bushes, a ditch for scooping up minnows, and woods and ponds to explore.

Leaving Georgia was hard, especially to move to the hot spot of the US. Life in Los Angeles was everything people had said it would be: plastic, beautiful, and surreal. The ocean view was nice, but it didn't make up for the friendlessness. I cared so much what people thought of me that I couldn't let my guard down and be who God made me.

Germany was no present to me either when we moved there, just before my thirteenth birthday, in the scorching summer of 2006. Then I met others from all over and found new perspectives. I met people who helped shape me into the girl I am today and helped me discover that there is no such thing as a nobody.

I enjoy moving around and seeing new sights. It has opened my eyes to all the somebodies and their lifestyles and how they each learn, grow, dress, and express themselves differently. The world is full of beautiful cultures, and I can't wait to see more, even in my own country.

There is no way for me to choose one of the places I've lived or seen to be my definite home. I've heard it said that "Home is where the heart is" and "Home is where the military sends you." I agree with both. Home for me is wherever I am at the moment or wherever my family is.

If I had to choose one place where I have grown the most and taken as part of my personality, for now I would choose Germany. Here, I have met my best friends and learned my most important life lessons—maybe because of my amazing surroundings or simply as part of my teenage growing years. Leaving Germany this summer will be one of the hardest moves, but one of the most important moves as well.

This fall I'll return to California—this time knowing that I am somebody—to study graphic design at Azusa Pacific University. I have gone from being a nobody to knowing who I am and what I want to do with my life.

Five years ago, if asked about my future, I might have made up some rigmarole about a conventional field of study. Now, I don't even have to think before I ramble on about what I want to do.

Art is my forte. I've always been an artist, whether through painting, drawing, fashion, or music. Art to me is seeing the potential in something and making it real. Maybe that includes the potential in myself.

Who knew becoming "somebody" could be so much fun?

★ ★ ★

Silver and Gold: A Circle of Friends

September 7, 2010

"Make new friends, but keep the old. One is silver and the other gold."

We were a small family in a big city—a strange place that was our new home but felt like the far side of the moon.

We slouched at a table in an unfamiliar restaurant. It was August in the desert Southwest. Drained from the heat and the day's disappointments, we looked without enthusiasm at the glossy menu.

Just returned from Guam, we had visited family in various states, then had driven two days across three more states to our new assignment: two adults, two cars, one air conditioner, a baby, a preschooler, the usual kiddie gear, lots of luggage, disposable diapers, and great expectations.

Earlier that day, we had arrived at the base with high hopes about our new home. We soon discovered our sponsor was on leave, and no one else knew we were coming. Promised reservations for temporary quarters had been forgotten, along with invitations to dinner.

Assurances that we would get military housing preference after our overseas tour also proved hollow. The housing office informed us that Guam, a US territory, didn't qualify as an overseas assignment. Several thousand miles of ocean and fifteen-hour plane trips that separated us from our loved ones while we were there were dismissed as irrelevant.

We were having a rough day, and we anticipated that more rough days lay ahead.

Frustrated, worried, and tired, I saw a bright-eyed, attractive mom with two young boys preparing to leave the restaurant. I turned my head, ashamed of my travel-frayed appearance.

Much to my dismay, she stopped at our table and spoke to us. But my self-conscious thoughts vanished when I heard her question. It was so unexpected because we thought no one knew we were there—or cared.

"Are you the Barnes family?"

In answer to our stunned looks and stammered affirmatives, she explained that her husband, Scott, had met us earlier that day. He worked in my husband's office, and had suggested a nearby hotel and the restaurant. He had to work that evening, and their boys had baseball practice, but he apologized and said they would have us over soon. Nancy repeated that invitation.

We accepted—repeatedly. After several months, we moved on base. Scott and Nancy and their sons became our near neighbors and dear friends.

Two years later, they moved, as military families do. Sixteen years later they remain our treasured friends.

"... A fire burns bright. It warms the heart. We've been friends from the very start."

A couple of weeks ago, we went to our favorite restaurant in a familiar German village—one that was once our home. The August weather was perfect, so we sat outside. We knew the menu by heart, but we looked at it anyway for old times' sake.

Wistfully, we named friends who used to eat there with us, but who have moved, as military families do.

Another family, new to Germany, finally found a home after two months of house hunting. Driving through their new village—our old one—they decided to stop at an unfamiliar restaurant, just as our food arrived.

My husband saw them drive up and said, "You won't believe who's here." It was Gail and Jim, who were our friends and neighbors in California five years ago.

We greeted them with big hugs at that little restaurant, in a place where they thought no one knew they were there—or cared.

"... A circle's round. It has no end. That's how long I want to be your friend."

★ ★ ★

What Goes Around Comes Around

November 23, 2010

With a nod to Laura Numeroff, author of *If You Give a Mouse A Cookie*: When you give a neighbor a plate of cookies, she'll probably give some to her family. If her family likes them, chances are, she will ask you for the recipe. Then she might make some, too.

When she bakes a batch of cookies, it's likely she will give some to another neighbor, who will share them with her family, who will probably request tall glasses of milk to go with their cookies. After she finishes pouring the milk, she will probably call and ask for the recipe, too.

When these neighbors get orders to other assignments, possibly they'll take the recipe with them. After unpacking their mixers, pans, and spatulas, they might make plates of cookies for their new neighbors, who will then get busy pouring milk and asking for the recipe, too.

When they ask for the recipe, these neighbors might ask each other more questions, like "How old are your children?" and "Who's your dentist?" and "Want to come over for coffee?"

If the answer to the last question is "Yes," then it's likely someone will bake cookies to go with the coffee.

If you repeat this process many times, in many places, with enough military friends, your recipe could travel around the world, even to places you've never been.

Then one day, years later, when your oldest child is far from home—across the ocean, in fact—someone who got the recipe from her mother, who got it from you, might just show up at your son's door with a plate of cookies for his birthday.

At least, that's what happened to me.

When I wrote about baking pumpkin cookies in October, I received messages from as far away as Pearl Harbor and Dubai.

Here's a taste:

Linny in Nebraska: "I tripled the recipe and made cookies for the neighbors. Everyone loved them and asked for the recipe. Thanks for sharing your fall tradition with us." Linny's daughter Gwynne in Virginia sent a picture of her batch of pumpkin cookies.

Leslie in London: "Making the cookies today."

Nancy in Louisiana: "Friends I shared with wanted the recipe, too. One friend said they were so good I could sell them, but I only bake for love not money!"

Dawn in Germany: "Made your pumpkin cookies for my stairwell today. Yummmm-o!"

Joanne in Korea: "We were talking about cookies at work, and mentioned that I had seen a pumpkin cookie recipe ... I am headed to the commissary to get the ingredients to bake pumpkin cookies this weekend for my staff!"

Sheila in Georgia: "I am cooking them now ..."

Vickey in Germany: "I've heard so much about these pumpkin cookies that I'd like to try them, also. If you would like to pass along the recipe, I'd be a very happy gal!"

Joel in San Antonio, Texas: "Forget the recipe. Can you drop some by my house?"

College son (Will) in Waco, Texas: "Send cookies."

Sad mom (me) in Germany: "If I mailed these cookies, you'd have to eat them out of the box with a spoon."

Dana (who got the recipe from her mother, who got it from me) also in Waco, Texas: "YAY!!! I am going to make some for your son for his birthday!"

Like I said, when you give a neighbor a plate of cookies, you never know where they might turn up.

~

Dear Terri,

Thank you so much for sharing your wonderful column.

I'm very honored that you used my story as a springboard! It was also very touching!

I spent a few days at a military base in Oklahoma and saw what life was like. I was treated like a celebrity, and I stayed in the beautiful building where the "big-wigs" stay, generals, etc.

My first morning there I woke up early and heard "Reveille" being played ... It was a fascinating visit! —Laura Numeroff

~

Pumpkin Cookies

(I did not create this recipe, nor do I know the origin. It was given to my mom by a friend who was also a military spouse, about thirty-five years ago.—tlb)

1 cup shortening	2 cups flour
1 cup sugar	1 teaspoon baking soda
1 cup canned pumpkin	1 teaspoon baking powder
1 egg	2 teaspoons cinnamon
1 teaspoon vanilla	1/2 teaspoon salt

Cream shortening and sugar, add egg and pumpkin. Add dry ingredients and vanilla. Mix thoroughly. Drop by tablespoonfuls on ungreased baking sheet. Bake 12 to 14 minutes at 350°, until cookie springs back when touched lightly in the middle. Let cool before frosting.

Caramel Frosting:
3 tablespoons butter
4 tablespoons milk
1/2 cup light brown sugar, packed
1 cup powdered sugar
1 teaspoon vanilla

Melt butter in sauce pan. Add milk and brown sugar. Stir until combined. Boil 2 minutes. Pour into mixing bowl and let it cool but not get completely cold. Add powdered sugar and vanilla. Beat until smooth.

(I use the 29-oz can of pumpkin, approximately 3 cups, and triple everything else.—tlb)

★　★　★

The 411:
Facts of Military Life

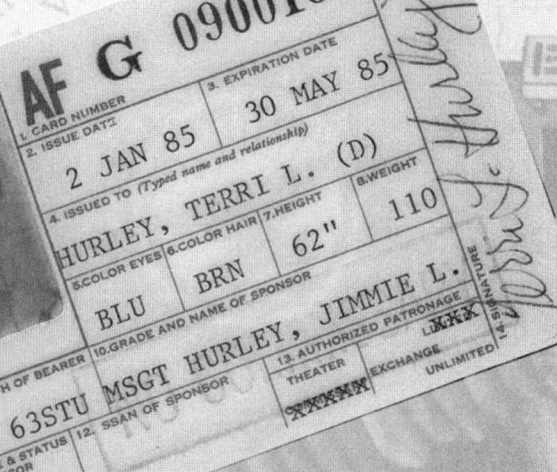

Trial by Fire

November 9, 2010

Imagine that a hundred houses in one neighborhood caught fire and burned to the ground, destroying most of the possessions of the families who lived in them. Furniture, clothing, bicycles, wedding albums, crayon drawings, all gone.

That's what happened in my neighborhood in Germany ten days ago. Fire destroyed a moving company warehouse outside Stuttgart and with it, the belongings of ninety-seven families transitioning in or out of the community.

Their houses were not destroyed, because these families don't have houses right now. These were families of military members and Department of Defense civilians.

These moms and dads, sons and daughters, pack up their lives and make a home wherever they go: curtains from the exchange, paintings made by the kids in grade school, a bedroom suite that's been around since newlywed days. Even the plain white walls of military quarters take on the character of the occupants when their lives are unpacked and settled there.

As military families, we regularly watch strangers from a moving company wrap up, crate up, and drive away with the worldly goods we use to create the atmosphere we call home. We wave goodbye, and we know the risks when the truck pulls away. We might never see any of it again.

"It's just stuff," we say to ourselves and our friends. We learn to hold it loosely. What else can we do?

We know what can happen, but more often than not, most of our stuff shows up again—perhaps a bit more travel-worn—ready to be reassembled into the home we love, wherever Uncle Sam sends us. We rejoice in spite of the dents and scratches.

For these families, the unthinkable happened when fifty thousand square feet of personal possessions went up in flames.

"No it's not *just stuff,*" wrote one friend after hearing the news. "A baby box is not *just stuff.*"

She's right. Stuff is what is available at the local department store: a sofa, a blender, towels, silverware, underwear.

Treasures are irreplaceable. Made by a daughter, given by a grandmother, discovered at a flea market, treasures don't have a price tag. They hold memories too priceless for the "replacement value" provisions of an insurance policy.

Patty, an Army wife, just moved here to Germany with her husband. Their home was packed up and stored in that warehouse, waiting for their move-in date. I saw her at the post exchange the other day. She was making a price list for the claim she and her husband will need to file to be reimbursed for their losses.

Her outlook was positive. She smiled and said there are worse things. No lives were lost. She talked about meeting other families who had lost their possessions to the fire and expressed sympathy for the families with young children. Her children are grown.

Then she sighed and said, "Even if it's charred, I would like to have one baby picture."

Our community has mobilized to help those who have lost everything on the cusp of the holiday season.

The Stuttgart USO and Army Community Services are coordinating donations. The spouses club and the chapel community are also stepping up to help. Fellow military families here and at other installations began offering clothing, furniture, and funds as word spread of the calamity.

Memories are indestructible, even if scrapbooks are not. No one can replace everything that was lost. We can only hope and pray that the generosity of friends and strangers will write a new chapter of memories for these families to keep.

★　★　★

The Real Thing?

October 4, 2011

She's not a real military spouse, but she plays one on television. Kim Delaney, arguably the biggest star of Lifetime's *Army Wives*, was asked to speak at a gala event honoring former Secretary of Defense Robert Gates a week or two ago. Unable to read or remember her prepared remarks about military life, the confused actress was gently escorted from the stage, looking like a lost child.

She may have been under the influence of an unknown substance or simply sabotaged by a faulty teleprompter, but she did not project the elegant confidence of Claudia Joy Holden, her *Army Wives* character.

Whatever the reason for her odd behavior, I'm not joining the attack on Delaney. Heaven and *The Huffington Post* know she must be humiliated enough. Her embarrassing moment has been shown on television, reviewed online, and reviled by YouTubers.

Perhaps the blame lies with whoever asked an actress— even an Emmy-winner like Delaney—to talk about being a military spouse. When was the last time anyone asked a military spouse to discuss the acting life?

If I find something worthy of criticism rather than pity, it is the culture of celebrity that confuses stardom with expertise, and invites a make-believe military spouse to talk about a life she only knows through scripted scenes.

I applaud the entertainment industry for noticing that military spouses are out here. At least *Army Wives*—if not exactly reflective of our real lives—does attempt to tell our tales in soap-operatic style. We bask in the knowledge that our lives are worthy of exaggeration and glorification, Hollywood's sincerest forms of flattery.

As an added attraction, the popular program has produced glamorous celebrity versions of ourselves. When those celebrities begin to represent us in real life, that's when the applause light goes off for me.

So I pose the same question I heard from others in the blogosphere: Why wasn't a real military spouse invited instead?

The ceremony to award the Liberty Medal to Gates included video tributes from three former presidents, a former Supreme Court justice, and the secretary of state. Remarkably, no one asked any cast members from *The West Wing* for their input.

I can easily think of several real military spouses who turned their own obstacles into stepping stones for the rest of us, and who would have been excellent representatives.

How about Army wife Tawny Campbell, who founded Project TLC while stationed in Germany? Her trio of charities serves wounded warriors, deploying troops, and their families with letters, Christmas gifts, and free family portraits. The mother of two young children has operated the nonprofit program since 2007, even when her husband was deployed, with help from volunteers worldwide.

Then there's Bonnie Carroll. After her military husband died in a plane crash in 1992, she founded the Tragedy Assistance Program for Survivors. Since then, TAPS, with Bonnie as president, has served bereaved military families with resources and information, casualty assistance, and support programs, including "Good Grief Camps" for the children of fallen service members.

Or we could have heard from Heather Hebdon. A military wife now widowed and the mother of a child with Down syndrome, she founded Specialized Training of Military Parents in 1985—even before the military created the Exceptional Family Member Program to identify service family members with special needs. Now funded by the US Department of Education, STOMP is still helping military parents to find the best care and education for special needs children.

Come to think of it, maybe all the real Army wives were busy that night. They and their Marine, Air Force, Navy, Coast Guard, Guard, and Reserve counterparts are probably busy most nights—days, too.

Not all are at the helm of national organizations. Some are busy doing the work of two parents during deployment. They are attending parent-teacher conferences or Family Readiness Group meetings, maintaining a career, or caring for their own wounded warrior at home.

Some nights they might even get together with their friends to enjoy an episode of *Army Wives*. There is one thing they are not doing. They are not confusing what they see on television with the lives of real military families. The true stories are much more compelling.

★　★　★

Special Needs, Special Dad

February 15, 2013

Jeremy Hilton has testified for congressional committees and written for *Time* magazine, but he's neither politician nor pundit. He's been interviewed by network anchors and the ladies on *The View*, but he's neither business mogul nor movie idol. He's not the front man for a band, but he could be called a rock star.

Jeremy is an Air Force spouse and an advocate for military families with special needs, including his own family. He and his wife, Renae, have two children, Jack, 3, and Kate, 10. Kate has multiple disabilities.

A former submariner, Jeremy left the Navy to become a stay-at-home dad after Kate's birth. Her first five years were marked by multiple surgeries, thousands of hours spent in therapy, and doctors' appointments. All this as Renae's career followed the usual course: deployments, moves, transitions.

"We moved five times before Kate was seven," Jeremy said.

Two consecutive assignments in the Washington, DC, area provided the family some stability. Jeremy decided to put his hard-won knowledge and proximity to Capitol Hill to work as an advocate for military children like Kate.

"We went through all those transitions with her," he said. "We learned what it took and where the weak spots in our system exist. These are broken things. If I don't try to fix them, who's going to?"

Jeremy began speaking out for families like his, and his platform helped him become Armed Forces Insurance Military Spouse of the Year for 2012. The commercially-sponsored title, conferred by *Military Spouse* magazine, gave him national visibility, which he's used to advocate strengthening the support system for military families with special needs.

Jeremy said the system has community and military components, both in need of change, offering a few examples of a complex set of problems.

On the military side, he explains, Tricare covers most medical issues, but there is a whole spectrum of special needs not covered. For example, certain widely-used therapies for autism are classified as "educational" by Tricare and are not covered.

On the community side, military families often have difficulty accessing programs like Medicaid, because the services are wait-listed by state. Jeremy says that waiting list times are much longer than standard military assignments. When a family moves, they go to the bottom of the list in their new home state, further delaying care.

Those who assume that military healthcare and state benefits automatically cover all the needs of a disabled family member are not alone. Jeremy says government representatives don't have the whole picture either.

After a briefing about military families and state-based waiting lists, a Department of Health and Human Services representative told Jeremy, "I just hadn't thought about military families."

Words like these motivate Jeremy to communicate the urgency of the issues wherever he can, but changing the system via bureaucracy is slow, complicated, and frustrating.

"People are usually very open to this and want to help. They can say until they're blue in the face that they understand and that this is important," he said, spreading his hands, "but ... translating words into meaningful action is the challenge.

"It's my job to get the word out," he said. "What I'm trying to accomplish is to figure out ways to access what is available, so we aren't penalized for being military families. We're not asking for anything above what the civilian world has. We're asking for parity."

Although he speaks out for families like his, Jeremy recognizes his actions may not affect his daughter's care, because change happens slowly.

"But they're going to impact a lot of other children coming behind us," he said.

Aware of the parents caring for special needs kids who don't have the time or opportunity to speak out, he said, "Somebody's got to stick up for them."

★ ★ ★

We Were Thrifty Before It Was Nifty

July 17, 2011

Thrift shops are now vogue. Racks of used clothes are "vintage." Furniture with a few scrapes and tatty décor items well past their prime are "re-purposed."

It's all the rage to recycle and reuse. It's hip to hang out in thrift shops. Even my eighteen-year-old daughter and resident fashion maven loves them.

We military spouses were ahead of our time. We were buying and selling one another's "shabby chic" misfit curtains when our civilian counterparts were having their drapes custom made at Sears. Tres passé!

We were browsing through the cast-off toys and books from our friends and neighbors when everyone off base was at Kaybee Toys and Waldenbooks. Way off base.

When everyone else was saving a few cents at Blue Light Specials, military spouse club thrift shops were raising money in our communities and giving it away to libraries, scout troops, and college-bound students.

Blame it on hard economic times. The rest of America has realized what we've known for years: Thrift shops are treasure troves of the cheap and useful, bazaars of the bizarre and Bohemian—oh, make that "Boho."

Thrift shops on military installations are also centers for community news, and sometimes an offshoot of the local grapevine. You can find items and information you need and some you didn't know you needed. Take a stroll through your nearest spouse's club emporium and you may find:

Disney movies for a dime (or a whole bagful for a dollar); a glass pitcher just like your grandmother used to have; video games; a vacuum cleaner in need of some repair; oversized wooden spoon and fork, suitable for hanging—and a flyer for a basewide barbecue.

Chunky bracelets from the '80s; clip-on earrings that are even older; clothes for the dress-up box; a mounted deer's head;

a shelf for the garage; a miniature secretary desk (complete with pigeonholes)—and a little local gossip.

A Superman costume for Halloween and a plastic pumpkin to go with it; a petticoat; a sari; a dirndl; an obi; a lazy Susan from the Philippines; wine-tasting glasses from Provence; beer mugs from Munich—and an invitation to Bunco.

A silverware caddy for a quarter; a blow dryer for a buck (110 or 220, choose your voltage, depending on your next assignment); a designer blouse with tags still attached; a replacement carafe for your coffee maker—and advice on where to get your hair cut.

Baskets (with or without handles); bags (cloth, paper, and plastic); boxes (fabric, metal, or wood); balls (basket-, foot-, soccer or yarn)—and news about the neighborhood crafters and quilters groups.

Sunglasses, large and round or small and squinty; a floppy hat for sitting at the beach; a souvenir snow globe from somewhere you've never been—and maybe a conversation with a friend you haven't seen in a while.

Paperback books of every description; bird cages; a hamster cage with exercise wheel; kitty litter boxes; dog kennels, leashes, and collars—and the address of a good groomer.

A chubby lime green teapot with a blue lid; Coach handbags (authentic and otherwise); baby clothes; bibs and blankets; tennis racquets; snow skis and poles—and a chance meeting with someone you knew at a previous assignment.

Like the items on the shelves, the thrift store craze is nothing new. It has come and gone before. In a few years, boutique thrift stores may fade again, but like Goodwill and the Salvation Army, it's a safe bet that military spouses and our retail outlets to "re-purpose, recycle, and re-use" will soldier on.

We need a place to find the necessities of setting up housekeeping at each new assignment. We need a place to jettison our junk before an overseas move. We could make a collective killing on eBay. Instead, we will continue to donate or consign the clothes our kids have outgrown and the rugs custom made for the homes we've left behind.

One spouse's household purge produces another's priceless find. In our case, it also offers scholarships, new books, school supplies, and a great place to run into friends new and old—oh, make that "vintage."

★ ★ ★

Mrs. Doolittle

December 30, 2007

Jonna Doolittle Hoppes is not a military spouse, but her connection to spouses began with her grandmother, Josephine, the wife of General Jimmy Doolittle.

Jonna's grandfather, who led the Tokyo Raid four months after Pearl Harbor, received the Medal of Honor. Jonna says her grandmother was also a hero, one who served without rank or medals throughout her husband's long military career.

"I will always believe that my grandmother is a national hero," said Jonna from her home in California.

"My grandmother, like so many of her generation—no, let me rephrase that—like so many who chose to serve their country, including the men and women serving today, would never consider herself a hero," Jonna said, "but her selflessness is characteristic of a true hero."

"Part of her strength was her ability to let my grandfather do the things he needed to do, to allow him to 'fly' while providing a secure base for his launch and return," Jonna said. "But her gifts to those around her also contribute to my belief."

While her husband was away during WWII, Josephine Doolittle, known as "Joe," wrote a newspaper column for military wives. She also had her own radio program.

"During the war years, she spent her time writing and touring for the women who had loved ones fighting in Europe or the Pacific," Jonna said. "Then, during that last year of the war, she spent her time working with the boys returning from the front, those boys who were fighting the demons that accompany combat."

Jonna grew up as the granddaughter and daughter of career Air Force men. Her father, John Doolittle, followed his father's footsteps and was also a decorated combat pilot. Her mom, Priscilla, was a career military wife.

"My mother, like my grandmother, had the philosophy, 'Bloom where you are planted.' Every move was an adventure,"

Jonna remembers.

"We also learned that we had choices. You can either make the best or worst of each move. It is a basic tenet of my life that my attitude makes all the difference. I can choose to make the best of where I live, the people I work with, or any other facet of my life."

The lives of her grandparents have influenced her in other ways. In 2005, Jonna authored a book, *Calculated Risk: The Extraordinary Life of Jimmy Doolittle,* which she said she wrote from her grandmother's point of view.

Now she travels the world to tell people about her grandparents, preserving their memory and the history they helped make.

I met Jonna when she came to Germany to speak at a luncheon organized by the Ramstein Officers' Spouses Club. The luncheon was also a benefit, through sales of her book, for the Fisher Houses at Landstuhl Regional Medical Center.

She called the event a highlight of her trip to Europe. That experience, and the spouses she met, inspired her to seek opportunities for similar fundraising efforts, she said.

Above all, Jonna said she is continually inspired by her grandmother, who died in 1988.

"If the Egyptians are right and our souls are reincarnated until they become pure light, then my grandmother will not be back," Jonna said. "She has left a mark on many people, my mother, my sister, her friends, and me."

★ ★ ★

Spell It Out With Real Letters

November 11, 2007

On Veteran's Day 1998, Andrew Carroll made an appeal via Abigail Van Buren's column. While compiling the bestselling *Letters of a Nation*, published in 1997, Carroll said he was drawn to wartime correspondence. His "Dear Abby" request was for veterans and their families to send him letters written during war.

Nine years and 80,000 letters later, Carroll has published three books of wartime correspondence: *War Letters*, *Behind the Lines*, and *Grace Under Fire*.

I wondered what a letter enthusiast like Carroll would have to say to today's military families about staying in touch by mail. What does he think about email?

"I'm very sympathetic to the fact that email is quick and easy and allows families to stay in communication instantly," Carroll said by phone from his Washington, DC, office.

"There is some incredibly profound, dramatic, riveting, and extraordinary correspondence sent through the Internet. Having said that, what I encourage troops and loved ones to do every so often is to sit down and write a letter," he said.

"The implicit message of every handwritten letter is, 'You're worth the time.'"

Their tangible nature is also important.

"These letters are something people are going to hold on to and cherish. There's nothing like holding the actual paper your loved one handled as well," he said.

Preserving correspondence is another of Carroll's passions, one reason he created the Legacy Project to preserve the correspondence of military members, veterans, and their families.

"One thing I'm emphatic about is when you get an email, print it out," he said. "I hear people say 'Our computer crashed, we lost all of them,' because they forgot to take time to do it."

Carroll said printing an email is safer than saving it on a memory stick because technology changes.

"During the Vietnam War, a lot of soldiers did audio tapes, and that was great because their families could hear their voices," he said. "But over time, most of the tapes have disintegrated," and tape players are disappearing.

"Paper, ironically, is the most durable form of technology we have. ... We have letters from the Civil War and the Revolutionary War that are as pristine as the day they were written."

Others, not so pristine, are equally expressive.

"Some letters from Desert Storm still have a layer of sand. Some letters from the Civil War are splotched with mud and rain, because a young soldier was writing his letter under the shelter of a tree during a storm," he said.

Carroll's interest in US troops and their letters is more than historical. The Legacy Project is his ongoing effort to preserve wartime correspondence.

In our conversation, I found Carroll reticent about his contributions, but vocal about writing, especially by US troops.

"These young soldiers, sailors, airmen, and Marines may not be thinking about their grandchildren," he said. "But when they go into the attic, closet, or basement and come across these old letters, it's going to be an extraordinary way for these young people to connect with their grandparents."

~

Since this column was written, Andrew Carroll donated his collection of approximately 100,000 war letters to Chapman University in Orange, California, which created the Center for American War Letters. The center, inaugurated on Veteran's Day, 2013, is intended to be a resource for research as well as for the general public.

★ ★ ★

The Way Glenn Miller Played

March 8, 2011

The opening notes of "Moonlight Serenade" swirled across the theater as we found our seats. The house lights dimmed, and the curtain rose on a scene from 1940s America, though we were on the other side of the ocean and the millennium.

Twenty or so musicians played the signature tune, tuxedoed, bow tied, and seated behind fashion stands emblazoned in art deco lettering, "The World Famous Glenn Miller Orchestra."

Woodwinds wove the silken phrases, gently punctuated by trumpets and trombones. Drums and bass strummed softly, while the bandleader plied his skills on a Steinway grand piano. As the song ended, he picked up the microphone and spoke to the audience.

"Guten Abend, meine Damen und Herren. Sie haben gerade 'Moonlight Serenade' gehört und nun folgt unser nächstes Stück ..."

And we were off on an evening of swing that juxtaposed German narration with American WWII-era songs, their lyrics and arrangements faithfully performed by a European incarnation of a quintessentially American institution.

It was the antithesis of every war movie I'd ever seen. Some moments bordered on the surreal, for instance, when the vocal ensemble—their pronunciation only slightly trans-Atlantic—sang "Over There," a George M. Cohen standard from both world wars.

One phrase commands, "Send the word, send the word over there ... that the Yanks are comin', the Yanks are comin' ..."

Sure enough, there we were sitting in the fourth row.

A female vocalist created a poignant moment in light of past and present conflicts, crooning words penned by Charlie Chaplin:

"If you smile through your tears and sorrow; Smile and maybe tomorrow; You'll see the sun come shining through ..."

The musicians were pitch-perfect—stylistically and culturally—in tribute to the time and place in which the tunes were born. If the director made any jokes at US expense, we with our menu-based German skills were blithely ignorant.

We did have to stifle laughter at moments the local audience might not find humorous, like when the bandleader kicked off a number by counting off in English, with an accented "a one, anna two …" Shades of watching the Lawrence Welk show at my grandmother's house.

This is not the music of our generation, or even our parents'. It's the music of the Greatest Generation, the ones who fought their way across Europe. In that fight, the Allies dropped bombs on the very town where we sat listening to the way Glenn Miller played.

Some in the audience may have remembered the bombs, but most did not look old enough to have danced to this music when the swing craze swept Europe. Tapping feet, knowing smiles, and nodding heads showed appreciation and recognition, though no one got up to jitterbug even at the finale, "In the Mood."

This was a cultural event, a concert not a dance, and the history is worth recalling even without fancy footwork.

At the height of his career as a bandleader, Glenn Miller—too old to be drafted—joined the Army Air Forces. He led a military band that entertained US troops in Europe. Miller died in 1944 when the plane in which he was a passenger disappeared over the English Channel. His name and his music still travel the world.

On the way home after the concert, we talked about the irony of hearing "Over There" when we are "over here."

Ten years into another conflict, we speculated about the future. Will our grandchildren ever have the opportunity to visit a rebuilt, peaceful, and prosperous Kabul or Baghdad? If so, might they attend a concert celebrating American music of the early 2000s?

Like the song says, "I can dream, can't I?"

Hi Dear, I am a 61-year-old 100 percent disabled staff sergeant, and enjoy reading Stars and Stripes. *I read your column regularly. From 1976 to 1980, I was stationed at the USAG Augsburg. My German landlord and my family became very good friends, even after we moved into housing. Frau Reindol lost seven brothers during WWII, and Herr Reindol was captured and held in Greece. He never fired a shot during the war. Back to Glenn Miller: I gave them a two-record set, the Glenn Miller anniversary album. It was one of their prize possessions. Yes, they listened to all the big band sounds. I am from the Chicago area, so I do go past the Aragon where they all played. I have a picture of my uncle and family there after he came back from Italy.*

Blessings to all Peace,

Ed B.

★ ★ ★

Stay-at-Home Dads

March 16, 2009

When I started seeking out stay-at-home dads in the military, I half expected tales of lonely fathers—shunned by playgroup moms—pushing strollers and enduring pitying glances from camo-clad he-men.

Instead, I found dads who rise above the stereotype, not because they're worried much about what people think, but because they're focused on their families' well-being.

Jeff Pizanti, a Navy husband and former spouses' club president in Long Beach, California, said he was too busy to hear negative comments.

"As a stay-at-home dad, there is a fifty-fifty chance that people expect me to be either antisocial in general or specifically not want to participate in events that are traditionally for women or mothers: helping out with school functions, meeting with a group for coffee, having play dates," Jeff said. "I generally enjoy those activities ... especially ones involving baking or food."

Far from being discouraged by others' preconceived ideas, Navy husband John Avelis said he enjoys being with his toddler son and providing an example of full-time fatherhood to those who are unaware of such a thing.

"I like being able to educate," said John from his home in Virginia. "I like it when people see that I have this cute, happy, laughing kid, obviously doing very well and loving life."

Mike Clark, an Air Force husband in Germany, said family concerns are paramount. He and his wife always wanted one parent to be home with their children. Right now, Mike is that parent.

"We've always had that value throughout her career," he said. "If I worked, and when I worked, it was when she got home—anything to avoid daycare. It's always been more beneficial physically, mentally, and emotionally."

The decision for dad to stay home might depend on whose career provided the best support for the family or which parent is more career-oriented.

"Her career was a lot more important to her than mine was to me," said John.

"I enjoyed doing what I did, but it wasn't that much a part of who I was. So it was a pretty easy choice to make."

"Every few years you've got to re-evaluate what you're doing," Mike said, "and whoever's turn it is to do whatever is necessary for the family, that's what you do."

Thomas Litchford, a Navy dad in Rhode Island, said some of the pressure men feel could be self-imposed.

"They think they're supposed to be the ones out in the workforce making money and bringing home the big paycheck every week," he said.

"My actual experience is that people tell me they think it's really cool that I'm a stay-at-home dad," Thomas said. "I've had friends who have told me that they wish they had my life."

John hypothesized why he and other military dads are content at home.

"I think it's because we are flexible. (Military families) know that our life isn't 100 percent ours," he said. "We understand that circumstances will be beyond our control.

"If you're talking to men whose families have accepted that, you're going to find they're happy and contented ... You can either be flexible or go crazy."

Full-time parenting is challenging. The hours are long, laundry never ends, and personal time can be limited.

"It's a lot like any job," Jeff said. "Sometimes it's a lot of work, but the rewards are great."

"Think about the average person you know who's out there in the work force," Thomas said. "It's not the most fulfilling thing. To have the opposite alternative, the opportunity to stay at home and raise your kids—that's pretty fulfilling."

★ ★ ★

Macho, Macho Spouse

June 21, 2013

For nearly a decade, Chris Pape didn't think much about being married to the military. He was proud of his wife's career in the Air Force and her service to the country, but he didn't consider himself part of the military community.

He considered himself a regular guy living a regular life. Sure, his wife's career took him to a new place every couple of years. Sometimes she was deployed to combat zones, but he said, "When she was home, everything was normal ... She had her career, and I had mine."

Until he didn't have it anymore. In spite of all his experience as a video producer, after leaving a good job in Arkansas, Chris couldn't find a job after the couple PCSed to South Carolina in 2011. His career crisis brought home to him that his life as a military spouse, starting over every few years, might not be as normal as he thought.

"I was losing my identity one move at a time," he said. "According to society and family, I should be the one making the money here, but I'm not. I'm the guy sitting at home doing the dishes."

After finding little in the way of encouragement or advice for male military spouses, Chris decided to create a resource by seeking out other men who were married to the military and compiling video interviews with each one. He wanted to know their stories for his own benefit and share them for the benefit of others like him.

"I wish I would've kept track of my mileage," said Chris. "I went to twenty cities in twelve states in 2012," bringing home video interviews and insights from other male military spouses.

Tapping the web design expertise of Taurus James, another Air Force husband, Chris created the Macho Spouse website at www.MaleMilSpouse.com. The site is a home for his video interviews, links to blogs, and other support. Connection is the biggest benefit, he said.

"When I did my first interview," Chris said, "I felt like a weight had been lifted off my shoulders. I felt so good. This was in North Carolina, and I had about a three-hour drive home. I felt like I could run all the way. I finally found someone who understands me and gets me ... That was definitely the most exciting time in this project, that contact with other male spouses."

According to the Macho Spouse site, DoD estimates in 2010 put the number of men married to military members at nearly 190,000. The Macho Spouse site includes a global locator for men who want to add themselves and connect with other spouses.

Chris said he learned more last year through working on Macho Spouse than he learned in his first nine years as a military spouse. His wife, Dana, is learning, too.

"It's been beneficial for her, for me, and for our marriage," he said. "She's learning what I've been feeling over the last several years by listening to what these other guys are saying. ... She'll say, 'I'm about to cry. I had no idea this is what you were going through.'"

Addressing the needs of male spouses is not just about including them in spouse events, Chris said. Like women, some men who are military spouses want to participate and some don't. There is no one right way to reach out and support spouses of any gender.

"Even though we're all one group," he said, "we're a broad spectrum of people. I don't think one person can say what's best for all military spouses, or even the majority of military spouses. Guys are fiercely independent, and it would be wrong if I started telling people how they should live and what it takes for them to be happy."

Chris said he's building a wide range of information that he hopes will serve the spouse community, informing them about financial and mental health issues, as well as connecting spouses or sometimes just giving them a good laugh. He's not trying to do it alone and is looking for spouses who can contribute blogs, videos, and other types of expertise to the nonprofit venture.

He said it took him ten years to realize what he was missing and start looking for it. He wanted to create something that would be there for other guys when they started looking, too.

"They may not know they need it today, but eventually they're going to need a source of support, and I want to be ready for it."

★ ★ ★

Welcome to the Table

April 26, 2013

I saw her as I walked into the dining room at a military spouse conference: A lone woman at a table for eight. Young, stylish, and self-assured, she had toned arms that would make even Michelle Obama envious. She'd probably be more comfortable with someone her own age and fitness level, not me, I reasoned.

A buffet plate in each hand, I scanned the large room for another place to sit. I was about to veer left when our eyes met and she smiled. Too late to turn back now. I smiled back, approached her table, and asked if I could join her.

"Yes," she said, but her smile faded as I put down my dessert plate. "Oh, you brought cheesecake to the table after I resisted it."

That's right, I did, I thought, and I'm gonna eat it, too.

Out loud I only told her my name and asked hers, which was Lori.

The table filled quickly with several more women, who rounded out the table and filled the generation—and nutrition—gaps. Conversation flowed naturally on the usual subjects: How long have you been in? What branch? Children? Where are you stationed? Oh, my friend is there. Do you know … ?

The lunch agenda was group discussion, and it turned out that Lori, a Marine Corps wife, wanted advice.

"I'm new to all this," she said. "I've only been in the military world for a year. There's so much I don't know." Her main concern, she said, was getting to know other military spouses.

Several chimed in that military culture can be difficult to understand but is generally welcoming. All assured her that it takes a little time. Someone dropped a casual acronym into the conversation, and Lori asked what it meant.

"BG is brigadier general," explained the woman next to her.

"See, I don't even know that," Lori lamented, dropping her head. "I really need help."

In spite of her claim of inexperience, we learned that she is already active in the community at her new duty station. A college professor in her professional life, she volunteered to teach the newcomers' classes for incoming Marine Corps family members, as a way to learn the ropes herself.

Lori confessed to having an ulterior motive for her volunteerism, getting to know other new spouses and families, and hoping they will get to know her, too.

"I just need to know the best way to approach other military spouses," she said.

Those around the table began to offer the standard advice, which has become standard because it works most of the time: Join a group that interests you, such as a book club or running club. Take a yoga class. You'll meet people, and one of those people could become the friend you can call at 2:00 a.m.

"But not every group is as welcoming as this group," she said. "Some people don't want to talk to me, so they don't know what I have to offer."

Cue the exchange of knowing looks around the table. We've all been there. We tried to tell Lori that she is not alone in that experience, but the more we explained, the more she insisted that her situation is different.

Maybe it is. Even in the uniform world of military life, there's no one-size-fits-all formula for friendship. Not for me, not for Lori, not for anyone.

We encouraged her to focus on those who are accepting and let her circle of friends grow from there, but she was insistent: "How can I approach people who don't want to accept me?"

For that heart cry, we had no good answer. We've all been rejected, or maybe we've rejected someone else for some reason: Perhaps her husband is enlisted. Or she's an officer's wife. He drives an SUV, obviously doesn't care about the environment. She has too many tattoos. That one? Her arms are too perfect, and she doesn't eat cheesecake. There's a prejudice for every situation.

We didn't know what other guidance to give Lori in her quest for acceptance and friendship in military life. We told her everything we knew, and our advice was unchanged by anything we learned about Lori that day—including the fact that her Marine spouse is her wife.

★ ★ ★

Stars and Stripes Forever

November 22, 2011

I admit it. I watched the latest *Captain America* movie just to see one of my favorite stars. Not movie stars—*Stars and Stripes*, the newspaper.

Catharine Giordano, editorial researcher at the *Stars and Stripes* library and archive, gave me the inside scoop about the newspaper's cameo in the film. In the scene, a glamorous girl in uniform plants a kiss on the superhero after reading about his exploits in the paper.

Catharine knew about the role because the movie's prop crew got some guidance from the *Stripes* archive staff to create an authentic-looking paper for the movie's WWII setting.

It's all part of the job for Catharine and colleague Liliana Vivanco, guardians and maintainers of the colorful history of *Stars and Stripes* at the paper's headquarters in Washington, DC.

Catharine said *Stripes* has documented military life and history through the perspective of the active duty member.

The newspaper served brief stints in both the Civil War and WWI. Publication was revived again at the beginning of WWII and has continued daily ever since, distributed wherever troops—and their families—are stationed worldwide.

That's plenty of history to preserve and research. Past newspapers are maintained in various ways. The shelves of the *Stripes* library in DC hold print copies dating as far back as 1918. All editions since 1942 on are on microfilm. Newspapers as far back as 1948 have been digitized and archived online. Since 1999, *Stars and Stripes* daily content has been published online, but not all editions are available at a mouse click. That's where Catharine and Liliana come in.

"In this increasingly digital world, people come to expect to just Google and get it," said Catharine. But it's not that easy.

Getting the WWII years online and classifying them properly is an ongoing, complicated process, Catharine said, because so many editions were produced in those years.

"During WWII, we had over thirty different editions," said Catharine. "As the front changed throughout the war, new editions sprang up, and others closed."

As well as preserving *Stars and Stripes* history, Catharine and Liliana bring it into the present, fielding questions from reporters, TV producers, and individuals.

"A woman called because she thought we had a photo of her husband with Louis Armstrong," Lili said. "I was able to find it, so it was a happy ending."

Requests come from all over the world from families looking for news about a relative serving overseas, students seeking homework help, filmmakers and news outlets requesting information or photos.

Catharine said her most difficult assignments come from veterans needing evidence for benefit claims. A 1973 fire at the National Personnel Records Center in St. Louis, Missouri, destroyed large numbers of military discharge records from 1912 through 1964. For some veterans, a news story mentioning their service might provide the proof necessary to obtain VA benefits. The *Stripes* archive can help some but not all.

"Making that call that you tried everything, but were unable to find it never gets easy," said Catharine.

"I've also had German WWII babies, now grown, asking for help finding their American fathers and vets asking me to find a long lost love," Catharine said, adding that those requests are often beyond the scope of the newspaper's historical record.

She said research is the best part of her job, and she gets frustrated when films or publications cite *Stars and Stripes* as a source of information without verification.

"Then it is up to us here in the archives to gently tell all the people who inevitably call looking for that particular article or photo that we do not have it."

For example, she said, *Stars and Stripes* has no aerial photographs of Noah's Ark, "no matter what has been said in a documentary."

Armed with *Stripes* history and their research savvy, Catharine and Liliana can resurrect the past, help mild-mannered reporters in the present, and even lend a hand—or a newspaper—to a superhero.

"But," said Liliana, "we do not leap tall buildings."

★ ★ ★

Stand and Deliver

January 3, 2012

Exquisitely coiffed and elegantly clad, they glittered in formalwear and dress uniforms, every medal and ribbon in place. Their faces were expectant, polite, noncommittal.

They were there for a night out, a break from the kids, a meal they didn't have to prepare or carry out. Food and drink, prizes, music and dancing awaited them. The only thing standing between them and a good time was me.

Glancing down at my notes, I nearly bumped my nose on the mike.

I looked up, attempted a calm smile, and thought, "This would be less painful for all of us if I just put it in my column and let you read it with your morning coffee."

As always, when faced with a sea of faces, a microphone, and hieroglyphic notes that made sense yesterday, I asked myself: "Why did I say yes? I'm a writer, not a speaker."

Too late now—I did the only thing I could. I plunged.

"Thank you so much for inviting me to be here tonight to honor the military family ..." I was asked to be the speaker for a military ball because the theme for the night was military family and because the organizers were trusting souls.

I had prepared a few remarks about the things we experience in military life that we never thought we would do or could do—and even some of the things we hope we'll never have to do.

As an Air Force brat, I never thought I'd marry someone in the military. Now I'm so glad I did. My husband, sitting at the nearest table, smiled encouragingly. He's a seasoned speaker, knows what an introvert I am, and feels my pain.

Like most military family members, I've been to parts of the world I never dreamed I'd see, had experiences I never imagined: wonderful, painful, and downright miserable. If I'd known better, I might have tried to avoid some of them—like this one, perhaps.

I made a few weak attempts at humor and received polite

tittering. It seemed to come mostly from the people at my table, who would have to face me over dinner when I finished.

Eons passed, yet I was only halfway through my notes. I'd timed my remarks at barely over ten minutes, but surely I had aged ten years since I stood up. Aware of every gray hair on my head, I saw young wives in lovely dresses, sailors sharp in their dark blue crackerjacks, decorated Marines and soldiers who know firsthand about combat.

These are people who face deployment with wills written and funerals preplanned. What could I possibly say to them about the weight of risk and responsibility balanced with the rewards of the life they've chosen?

Wartime injuries change lives and end some. Budget cuts threaten benefits that help us make ends meet. We don't serve our country to make the Fortune 500, but we have to care for our families.

One war was recently declared "over." Other battlefronts remain. I don't know what the remainder of military life holds for my own family. How can I reassure a roomful of strangers that the good will outweigh the bad?

Perhaps risk and reward can't be balanced. How do you weigh the value of one against the other? In military life—in every life—we are called to do things we never wanted to do. We will choose either to do what is comfortable or what makes a difference.

Later, in the parking lot, a sailor about to get in his car spoke to us as we approached ours. "Thank you for what you said, ma'am," he said. "My wife and I really appreciated it."

Whether good intentions overcame poor delivery, or he was simply an exceptionally kind young man, I was grateful.

Fortunately, brilliant oratory is not required to remind military families what they already know about their lives: This life is costly beyond description. What it gives in return is not available at any price.

★ ★ ★

Military Moms

May 10, 2010

The three of us were laughing over chips and salsa in downtown Dallas, far from our families, our daily lives, and the war when Nancy's cell phone rang. She answered it and spoke to her husband, while Linny and I continued our lighthearted chatter at a slightly lower volume.

I glanced at Nancy during her phone conversation. She was near tears. After hanging up, she turned her attention back to us for a few minutes, saying little and dabbing surreptitiously at her eyes.

We continued talking for a short time, respecting her reserve, but it soon gave way. Abruptly, Nancy's eyes locked on mine and she said, "Mitchell is going to the war." Her tears fell freely then—tears of concern for her youngest son.

I could only grab her hand in sympathy. Linny, whose son served in Iraq with the Army, took each of us by the hand and said, "We're praying right now." And we did, drawing curious glances from nearby diners at the busy restaurant.

Mitchell and my oldest son were cowboys together—also Transformers, Batman and Robin—when they were preschoolers and our families were stationed at the same Air Force base. Now grown up and an airman, Mitchell awaits orders to serve in the same war his father joined at its beginning.

On September 11, 2001, his mother and I pondered the tragedies over the phone, hours after the attacks. We wondered together that day how such terrible things could happen and when—not if—our military husbands would be summoned to the conflict.

Soon they were. We were not stationed at the same base then, but we were close enough that Nancy and I and our kids could spend occasional weekends together while our husbands were gone. We were strong for each other and even more so for our children, then and through several more deployments.

When I first met Linny, another military wife, her son was serving in Iraq. She gave a small card with his picture, name, and address to me and to other friends, asking us to pray for him during his deployment. We did.

He returned safely and was preparing to process out of the Army in the fall of 2009. On the morning of November 5, he'd planned to be at the Fort Hood Soldier Readiness Center, but overslept. Later, he called to let his family know he was okay after a soldier-turned-terrorist killed thirteen and injured many more that day.

Linny said that event was worse than any deployment.

"In Iraq, you kind of expect that there are bad guys out there," she said. "When they're on their base at Fort Hood, Texas, you think they're safe."

Linny said she realized her days as her son's protector were over the day he left to join the Army.

"He had to go off and be a man," she said. "I felt like my heart was being yanked out of me."

When she first saw her son after boot camp, she recognized the transformation from little boy to confident young man.

"He's chiseled and has this bright smile," Linny said. "You know that he has gone through some tough times and he has come through just shining, confident."

That reassured her that he was prepared for deployment. Nancy said she and her husband have complete confidence in Mitchell's training also, though letting go is difficult.

Linny's advice to military moms like Nancy, particularly during deployment, is to depend on a small group of understanding friends for prayer and support.

I'm already signed up for that duty. Nancy and I, true to our friendship and our military-wife experiences, will be strong for each other, our husbands, and our children.

★　★　★

ID Cards and My True Colors

May 2, 2010

It's the priceless item that validates our identity as military dependents, a passport to all things military, allowing military spouses to bloom where we're planted all over the world: the military identification card.

Without it, we are persona non grata at any US installation. With it, the world of commissary and exchange privileges, cheap movies, crystal bingo, bowling, and military medical care are open to us.

I've had a military ID for most of my life, first as a daughter and now as a wife.

I still have the last ID card from my dependent child days. Fret not security-minded individuals; the card is invalidated by a strategically punched hole—very OPSEC. Plus, it looks less authentic than what any ten-year-old could make with a laptop these days. It looks more like a membership card for the Cap'n Crunch Club, free in specially marked boxes, than a current high-tech ID.

My old card was revoked when I graduated from college. It was a sad day—the revoking, not the graduating.

When I got married, it seemed unjust that my new husband, then a reservist, could have an ID card, while I—with twenty-one years of seniority in military life—did not qualify. I could only shop on base when he was with me to make the purchases and show his ID card. Talk about dependent.

A few years later, my husband went on active duty. The military world welcomed me back with open arms—and a new ID card—as a true "dependent." I've had twenty-one years' worth of IDs since then.

When I was a kid, the worst part of getting an ID was the uncertainty. ID card pictures are notoriously unflattering. In the days before instant digital photography, they were also unpredictable. One shot, no previews, no choices, no retakes, followed by weeks of suspense while the card was processing.

Whatever the results—flattering or not—the die was cast until the card expired.

My mom had an ID card photo for several years that caught her with her tongue out. The photographer snapped the picture while Mom—preparing for the photo—was moistening her lips. Mom used to joke about sticking out her tongue at commissary cashiers so they would recognize her at the checkout. She was glad when that one expired.

Now that I'm an adult, the worst part of renewing an ID card is facing tough questions like: "How much do you really weigh?" and "What color is your hair?"

I had to get a new ID card the other day. The people at Pass and ID were friendly and helpful, but nosy.

"Your information says you're blonde," said the cute thirty-something clerk, looking at her computer. "Do you want to change that, or are you planning to color your hair again?"

"No, this is my natural color. I won't be changing it," I said, slightly confused.

She looked puzzled, too, and then I realized her implication was that my natural color, perhaps more silver than gold these days, did not fit her idea of blonde.

She had already asked my age and weight, and I answered truthfully. So I thought she was pressing her luck a bit.

Noting her golden locks and brown roots, I considered telling her that I was more blonde than she was, but my better nature prevailed. Instead, I laughed and said, "Let me call it blonde for a little while longer."

She laughed, too, and humored me. Wow, I should have said 115 pounds. Maybe she would have let me get by with that, too.

★ ★ ★

Area Codes:
Moving and Travel

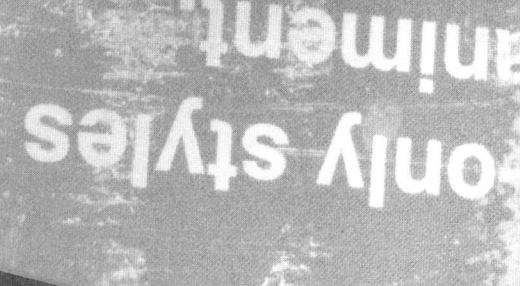

Empty Houses

June 22, 2008

The packing was done, the moving truck gone, and the cleaning finished. I walked down the stairs, averting my eyes from the bare walls where our children's faces used to smile down from framed family photos and vacation snapshots.

I stepped into the hall where the rug used to be. That irritating rug never would lie flat. I nearly tripped over it a hundred times, but I wished for a hundred more. In the kitchen, curtainless windows made the room look unusually bright—bright, clean, and empty.

A couple of weeks and a few thousand miles later, we walked into another house. The kids ran upstairs, eager to see the bedrooms and divvy them up. Their voices echoed down the hallway. A new house in a new neighborhood. Shiny clean floors and white walls—white, clean, and empty.

A new beginning. Another house to fill. How can something so empty be so heavy? I felt the weight of all I would need to do to make this hollow place into our home.

A few months later, I sat on the stairs in my neighbor's house talking to her and holding her new baby girl. We sat on the stairs because there was no other place to sit. The furniture was long gone, and the house was empty.

Everything was perfect for the housing inspection that day, but way too clean for real life. No Cheerios on the floor or crayon on the walls. All traces of the family who lived here were gone. Soon the family would be gone, too.

I'm beginning to hate clean, empty houses. I have seen too many of them. A few assignments ago, it was easier to start all over. Each move adds names to our Christmas list and pictures to the scrapbook, but it leaves an empty feeling that grows harder to fill each time.

I erase one street number and city from my address book to write a new one. Eventually the paper is worn out and won't hold another address. Some spaces just have to stay empty.

But the emptiness reminds me of what used to be there: the imprint of so many names and places that I can't list them all. They have left their mark. I could work frantically to fill in every blank, trying to get rid of the empty feeling, but some empty spaces have to stay that way. It leaves room for what I can remember, but can't carry with me.

That doesn't mean I'd leave my whole house empty in memory of what used to be. I could carry on like a low-budget Solomon, moaning about the futility of unpacking only to repack in a year or two, but I wouldn't have much of a life if I left all the cupboards bare and lived out of cardboard boxes.

This morning, when I was out walking through the neighborhood, I saw more empty houses. Today, they don't make me as sad as they used to. At one empty house, a full minivan stood in the driveway. A mom unloaded it while her children played in the garage.

Their moving truck will come soon. They'll empty their boxes and fill the house. Maybe a little bare space will remain, a little sadness for what's left behind, but maybe it has to be that way. Some spaces are filled and some remain empty, a reminder of the fullness of other places and other days.

~

Dear Terri,

I so enjoyed your article in Stars and Stripes. *I, too, was an Army wife, as we used to say in the British Forces. That was over forty years ago, and I know the trauma of moving house after house. We had four children, two boys and two girls.*

I went alone to Germany with two very young children. In those days (we traveled) by train, boat, and train again in deep snow. My husband met us at the train station to tell us he was off that night on a training exercise for two weeks. Welcome to Germany. But we loved it.

When we moved six years later, we had two more children. I never wanted to move again. But there were many more moves to come. It did affect the children's schooling. But my eldest daughter took it all in her stride and has ended up as head of a school here in England.

You don't know how much I missed the life when it was all over. My husband at 77 years still lives Army. I miss the moving, packing, and repacking.

Don't worry about the children. They do adapt. All ours have good careers but none wanted to follow their Dad.

Best wishes to all military wives. I wish it was me.

—S.M.

★ ★ ★

Small World

August 23, 2009

When we moved from Georgia to California a couple of assignments ago, we drove cross-country to our new home—with stops in Louisiana, Oklahoma, Colorado, Nevada, and a few other states. We visited military friends at almost every stop.

When we arrived in California, I told my new neighbor in base housing about our trek.

"Leaving Georgia was hard for our kids," I said. "I think this trip was good for them, because they saw that we can keep the friends we leave behind. Then they know when we say goodbye, it's not forever."

She looked at me blankly and said, "Oh, really? I thought it was."

I didn't know what to say. I didn't know anyone could survive a transient military life without staying connected to the people who become part of our lives at each assignment.

Another day, about two years later, I was driving down Pacific Coast Highway when my cell phone rang. I was on my way to get my international driver's license in preparation for our next move—to Germany.

It was my friend Nancy calling from Louisiana. Knowing about our upcoming move, Nancy, an Air Force wife, called to tell me about another military friend of hers, Sheila, whose family was also moving to Germany.

When we arrived there, we found that Sheila and her family lived down the street from us. We became close friends, sharing sporting events, holidays, and many milestones.

Sheila introduced me to Bonnie and Kelly, and we became a regular foursome for lunchtime celebrations of our birthdays or just being together.

Old friendships beget new ones and provide comfort when you haven't made new friends yet. The world seems smaller when your friendships stretch around the globe.

I'm a military brat from a military town. My daughter had

a middle school friend in Germany whose family had been stationed in my hometown. She attended the elementary school where my sister is a fourth-grade teacher. I told her my sister's name, and the girl exclaimed, "She was my favorite teacher ever!" Small world.

I'm visiting home now, sipping cappuccino in my favorite coffee shop.

The new barista, Janie, is a young Air Force wife. She's really a teacher, but her husband is only here for four months of pilot training. She decided to utilize her 'espressive' talents rather than complain about having nothing to do in this small farm town.

As we chatted, the owner of the coffee shop and another customer joined in. We found we each had a military connection: one retired airman, a widow of a civil service employee, and two military wives.

"You don't have an accent at all," said a customer to Janie after learning she came from Ohio by way of Tennessee. Traveling smoothes the edges off those regional distinctions, we agreed.

When this column goes to press, we'll be back in Germany—in a new assignment and a new home. In some ways, we're starting over again, but not really. We don't wipe the slate clean when we move, and thank heaven for that.

The sad goodbyes of our recent move are still fresh, but the comfort of friendship is worth it, even when the friends are no longer nearby.

Cleaning out cabinets in preparation for this move, I rediscovered the nursery music box used by all of our babies. I wound it up, and as I listened, I realized how appropriate the tune was for our three military children. The tune played, and the words ran through my head: "It's a small world after all."

With friends all over, yes, it is.

★　★　★

Not the Real Me

September 13, 2009

This is not me. It's not like me to be on the verge of tears during open house at my daughter's new high school. I'm a grown woman. People write me for advice, for encouragement. This week, I dispensed my wisdom via newsprint, email, and blog on BAH, TDY, and PTSD. A veritable alphabet soup of military spouse expertise, that's me.

This is not me: Sitting in the gymnasium, surrounded by parents I don't know; envying the moms who are greeting their friends after a summer's absence, sharing their latest travel adventures; listening to the principal talk about what a wonderful school year we are going to have.

Walking through unfamiliar hallways looking for my daughter and her Accounting I classroom, I feel lost and overwhelmed, especially knowing that my children face this every day at their new schools.

I've been a military wife for twenty-four years, through ten moves and four overseas assignments. I should have this down cold. I thought I did. Another move? No problem. Pack out, clean up, travel, travel, travel, unpack, hang curtains, join clubs, get involved. No whining, no pining for the halcyon days "at our last base."

Yeah, I've got all the answers. Bloom where you're planted. It's a small world and all that jazz. Instead, I feel small, while the world is huge. What happened to all that pre-move optimism? Like the queen-size sheets and enough room for all my shoes, I can't seem to find it.

This was supposed to be an easy move. That's what everyone said. We just moved a couple hundred miles down the road. Everyone assured me it would be a piece of cake. I was blindsided.

When it comes to leaving your friends and all that is familiar, two hundred miles might as well be two thousand. New school, new neighborhood, new friends—none of these are respecters of proximity. New is new. A move is a move, and by any other name, it still doesn't smell so sweet.

Not at first, anyway. I keep reminding my children that the first few weeks at any new place are the hardest.

"Give it time," I say. "Remember our last move? It wasn't much fun at first either, and then we loved it. This will be the same. It will get better."

So I keep giving myself the same advice. The unpacking will finally be finished. The strange will become the familiar, and I'll stop feeling so homesick for a place I called home for three years. The friends, however, I'll hold on to.

In our new home, I am meeting people. I do see an occasional familiar face or two at the commissary or at chapel. I know the seeds are there, and I will bloom where I've been transplanted once again. I am a resilient military spouse, after all. I know it. I just don't feel it yet.

Filmmaker Donna Musil, who created *Brats: Our Journey Home*, has strong feelings about the long-term effects of military life, including moving. She told me that she thinks extolling resilience "is the equivalent of 'get over it.'"

Resilience is necessary to survive any life, military or otherwise. However, I agree with Donna. "Get over it" is a retort, not a remedy.

When it comes to moving, I guess, practice does not make perfect. Being uprooted is painful every time, and there are no easy answers. I may not get over it, but I will get through it.

And that is me.

~

Dear Terri,

I read your article on 13 September, and I have to say, it seemed like you were writing about me! Although my husband is retired, we are still moving around with his job for the Air Force ...

Having moved with my dad as a child, and then thirty-three years as a spouse, I know all of the usual verbiage that accompanies PCS moves: "Grow where you're planted," "Give it time," ... blah, blah, blah. I've probably snottily spouted off more than my fair share of them when discussing a spouse who just can't seem to stop feeling blue about a move ...

Well, I know I'll get used to things the way they are, and like you, I'll bloom again where I'm planted, but I sure could use a hefty dose of Miracle-Gro right about now ...

Oddly enough, the older I get, the more difficult it is to pull up roots and start all over again. You'd think I'd be used to it by now, and able to just roll with the punches, but I've talked to several spouses, and we all feel the same way.

I just wanted to thank you for putting the feelings into words. It really helped me try to gain some perspective. ... Knowing that someone else is coming to terms with the feelings of loss and being blindsided by how "not easy" this whole thing is makes me feel a little less isolated. —D.

~

... Moving is painful and sucky and dirty and messy ... You know this, I know this, all those other wives know this. But the older ones know something the younger ones aren't supposed to know yet, because if they did they'd never move again: It doesn't get easier, and in a lot of cases, it gets worse, because we have more kids, more boxes, more furniture, sometimes more bills. Those who are moving without the kids they've sent to college know a whole other kind of pain ...

Yes, we'll get over it, through it, behind it (to hide in our weaker moments), and rise above it. In the meantime, though, there is the crackling tape of the boxes in our hearts that insist upon opening, and it's just another thing on the endless to-do list that is this life. —Diana Hartman

~

I got a knot in my stomach reading your September 13 column. I've been married for twenty years to my Navy husband. Just when I think I have it down, everything is running on autopilot, and the move was "easy," I get hit by that sense of loneliness.

It doesn't usually last long once I get involved in our new community, but it always temporarily returns—knowing I'll *never have my best and favorite friends all in one place, or the closeness of friends living overseas, and really knowing we can rely on each other.*

I still look forward to our future experiences and I cherish each new set of friends I make.

Thank you for your honesty! —CMW

~

WOW! This hit home with me today. We have recently PCSed to England from Germany, and I am once again wondering WHY ME? Where did I go? Amongst the boxes and organizing the house, taking kids to a new school, dinners, etc.

I am leaving behind a wonderful job. I try and remind myself it is not about me and my career, yet I had one and miss it terribly. So here I sit in the house being a housewife, which is as foreign to me as going to a new country.

I am trying to make my mark in England but, once again, I am starting at the bottom of people who are already here and established and YOUNGER!

You would think after twenty-two years of this, I would adjust. And, of course, I always do—I wouldn't be here if I didn't. I know how fortunate I am to have the opportunity to live this life. I just think it is good to have a sound-off board of other wives/ spouses who are in the tunnel with us.

I will walk with you through the tunnel, and just about the time we are out, we could be moving again. Thanks for your article—it made me smile! —LAT

~

Hi Terri,

My name is Dawn Penrod and I was just reading your article in today's Stars and Stripes, *and I have a strange question for you. Did you live [at Los Angeles Air Force Base]?*

If so, I think I sat next to you at Patch Open House last week … I thought it might have been you, but I thought I was looney tunes and did not say hello. However, after reading your column today I had to write.

So, if you are the same Terri Barnes, please accept my apologies for not saying hello ... If you are the same Terri Barnes and don't remember me, that's ok, but I wanted to extend a hello to you.

Mostly I wanted you to know that we all feel lonely in a new place. It will get better, I promise.

Sincerely,

Dawn

~

Author's Note: Yes, I am the same Terri Barnes that Dawn was talking about. Of course, I remembered her and wrote to tell her so. She invited me to coffee at her house the very next week. I was so busy feeling lonely in the crowd that I did not look up to see a friend sitting right beside me. Dawn's thoughtful note made me realize again that it is a small world after all.

★ ★ ★

Foreign

September 20, 2013

Being the new kid at school is nothing new for military kids like mine. As they've grown up, they've learned how to survive the initial discomfort of being strangers in a strange place. My youngest, Wesley, has just passed that stage at his latest school. A story he wrote for a class assignment reveals his best survival technique: Hope.

~

As I sit down in this new and unfamiliar environment, I take note of its residents. Everyone in the room looks at least two years older than me, and I know for certain I have never seen any of them before. This being a third year German class, I could very well be the only freshman here.

While the rest of the class files in, I do my best to fit in. Fitting in, as I observed the period before, entails sitting quietly, generally looking bored with life. Great, I can do that. The bell rings and the teacher begins her mildly patronizing spiel about her life and teaching style, with which I would soon become well acquainted. I soon find it much easier to keep up my "façade" of boredom.

It's been an hour since the class started. I haven't spoken to a soul, and no one has spoken to me. I am feeling about as foreign as the language I am trying to learn. The future of my fifth period class is looking bleak, and I begin to doze off. About halfway through a nice daydream of being somewhere else, the girl in front of me turns around and says:

"You're new here, right?"

Suppressing a heart attack, I shyly explained my situation. Dad's military. Moved. New. The girl told me that the kids in this class were all mostly freshman, and had been together since third grade. They were all part of a German immersion program to acclimate kids to the language, beginning in grade school. If I didn't feel like I was intruding before, I sure did after that. Thirty best friends in one class? How would I be accepted by them? Undoubtedly, I would be ostracized in every activity for the entire year. Fortunately, this was not the case.

Having attended only DoD schools until now, I didn't know what to expect. Hostility? Hardly. By the end of German 4, my sophomore year, the class contained some of my best friends. We bonded over our opinions of the beautiful and elegant German language, as well as a mutual disdain for our old German 3 teacher. I understood the inside jokes that had initially alienated me. I was accepted. I had a niche. And, most importantly, I had finally settled in and felt at home. When you move around a lot, like I do, it's very rare to find a group that you truly fit into, and I was grateful.

Arriving to my last class of the first day of junior year at another high school, I'm greeted again by the familiarity of the unfamiliar. Surveying the faces that surround me, I begin to wonder whether I'm the only upperclassman taking Algebra 2. The teacher begins to go over class rules and eventually assigns seats. Having the last name Barnes, I am naturally front and center, with the entire class looking at my back. Not wanting to attract any attention, I spend most of the class scribbling on my notes. After nine moves and many first days at new schools, I know how to look like I've got a grip on what's going on, whether I do or not.

I find myself tuning out most of what the teacher is saying in favor of staring at a speck of dust on the whiteboard directly in front of me. Anything is more interesting after hearing again the same speech I've heard in every class, about how misbehavior will not be tolerated. The teacher comes to the end of her monologue and lets the class talk amongst themselves. Ten minutes till class ends. With my backpack at my feet, I sit quietly. After about five minutes of sitting without a word, my intense examination of dust particles is interrupted by:

"Hey, aren't you new?"

* * *

Farewell to the Stairwell

May 24, 2011

For two years, our home has been behind door Number 2—in a "stairwell," the fondly used synecdoche for multi-family, multilevel military quarters.

When we moved into this four-apartment unit, our in-house neighbors included an Army family, a Navy family, and a Marine family. Our Air Force family completed the cross section of military services. If we'd had more space, we would have invited the Coast Guard. The more the merrier.

After a while, I grew accustomed to hearing the pitter-patter—sometimes stompity-stomp—of our neighbors' children. Then last spring, all three families PCSed at once. The building was suddenly still, echoing with only our own family's voices for a few weeks.

Then one morning in July, the stairwell resounded with deeper voices and much bigger feet. The household goods of our new top-floor neighbors and their four children were delivered to Number 4. A piano was unloaded, and someone played an impromptu concert on the sidewalk before the movers transported the instrument up the stairs.

I wrote on the Spouse Calls blog at the time: "I thought the return of next-door noise would annoy me. Maybe sometimes it will; I'm only human. But today, on a sunny summer morning, the sounds of movers tramping up and down the stairs and the new kids shouting excitedly to their parents are homey and familiar."

Within weeks, we had three new sets of neighbors. A dual military couple—Air Force and Navy—with two little girls moved into Number 1. A new Army family moved into Number 3, and before long, they added a new baby to their household of four. The stairwell was busy and buzzing once again with eight adults, a dozen kids, and one dog.

The piano music on move-in day proved prophetic. The children in Number 4 directly above us play various instruments, including the piano, guitar, and drums. A rock band practices at their house once or twice a week.

This sounds worse than it actually, well, sounds. For one thing, the band is pretty good, and for another, these are really sweet kids. If they see me returning from the commissary, they stop whatever they are doing and offer to carry grocery bags.

"Mrs. Barnes, if our music is too loud, please tell us," the guitarist son reminds me occasionally.

"Don't worry," I say. "We will."

And we do. My daughter, whose room is right below the practice room, hits the ceiling with a broom or whatever is handy when the volume level gets too high. Later, in the neighborhood carpool returning from youth group, she ribs her friends about disturbing the peace.

My stairwell neighbors are a near-at-hand source of eggs or chocolate chips when I run short in mid-recipe. Sometimes they also provide employment for our children, in the form of babysitting or dog walking. We exchange baked goods occasionally and meals when they're needed—one big happy family.

Okay, it's not all sweetness and light. There are times when I am tired of other people's noises, muddy tracks on the stairs, bikes, balls, and skateboards on the sidewalk. Our balcony is less than two feet from someone else's window. This is no treat for our neighbors either. I'm sure our patio conversations regularly invade their kitchen.

I admit I'm ready for a little more personal space and my own driveway. Soon I'll have it. Another turnover is beginning in our stairwell, and this time we're joining it. We are PCSing stateside to live in a single-family suburban home.

Someone is stomping up the stairs right now, and children are laughing outside. Will I be relieved or lonely behind my privacy fence and automatic garage door, no longer surrounded by the hubbub and camaraderie of other military families?

When he saw pictures of our future home in the US, our son asked, "That whole house is just for our family?"

After stairwell living, it looks like more space than we could possibly use. But I'm willing to give it a try.

★ ★ ★

Land of the Free,
Home of the Barnes Family

July 5, 2011

Crossing the Potomac at dusk, we saw the Washington Monument and the Capitol dome in the distance. This is a new place for our family, one where we've never lived nor even visited together, but its landmarks are well known to us. After five years of living overseas, we've come back home to America.

In our life as a military family, we've visited several world capitals. This is our first time in our own nation's capital, and we are not passing through on summer vacation.

Washington, DC, is my husband's latest assignment. Once again, our family is at home in a city that is new to us. This one is different. It's unfamiliar, yet full of images pictured in our history books and imprinted on our coins.

Our arrival coincided with the build-up to Independence Day. Flags flew everywhere. Summer tourists filled the downtown streets, buying t-shirts and taking pictures of their children in front of every monument.

I was one of them at first. Craning my neck for a first glimpse of the White House as we drove around the Ellipse, I felt like Jimmy Stewart in *Mr. Smith Goes to Washington*.

Since we arrived a few of weeks ago, we've been going here and there, getting our new life in order. I can't help saying, as we drive past various notable locations for the third or fourth time, "Look, you can see the (fill in the appropriate monument or memorial) from here."

One of my children usually reminds me, "We know, Mom, you told us."

Their young lives are crowded with iconic images from around the world. I was past thirty when our family began to travel the world together. I can't shake the awe factor, nor can I inspire it in my well-traveled children.

Crossing the English Channel for the first time last summer, I watched avidly from the ferry deck, eager for my first view of the storied White Cliffs of Dover.

When I spotted the thin white line on the horizon, the port of Calais was still visible behind us. I came back inside the cabin, where my family sat nonchalantly reading or napping, and said breathlessly, "Come out and look! From here you can see England and France!"

"And can you see someone's underpants?" quipped my oldest.

I convinced them all to come out and have their picture taken against the famous backdrop anyway, just like the tourists at the National Mall.

Perhaps living overseas has made us perpetual tourists, traveling everywhere, but not completely at home anywhere. On the other hand, in spite of being brand new to this city and not knowing much about it yet, I feel some sense of belonging.

The Washington Monument is visible from my window as I write. It rises in the distance, beyond the rooftops of base housing across the street. When I saw it the first time, I felt an odd mixture of familiarity and novelty—like turning the corner and seeing my mom's house after a long absence, combined with catching my first sight of the Colosseum.

Some new assignments feel like home sooner than others. I did not think this would be one of them. It's a large city in the East. I'm from a small town out West. Given that, and our far-flung life, I didn't expect this location to exert much gravitational pull. I can't explain why, but it does.

For the Fourth of July, we decided to eschew the enthusiastic crowds in the city center. More appealing to us was a neighborhood party on base, within walking distance of our family encampment in temporary quarters. Friends told us the famous fireworks would be visible from there, without the need to fight traffic or search for parking.

After all, we can go downtown during the off-season. We can explore museums and take in the significance of memorials and monuments after the crowds have abated.

For now, we may still be living out of suitcases, and yes, we still need the GPS to navigate the Beltway, but we're not tourists. We live here. We're home.

★ ★ ★

Traveling Exhibits of Our Past
August 30, 2011

"With all my worldly goods, I thee endow." When those old-fashioned words were spoken at our wedding ceremony, our combined possessions pretty much fit into my husband's little Mazda truck and my '65 Mustang coupe.

Last month, just weeks before our twenty-sixth anniversary, two moving trucks arrived at our house. Looking at the many crates about to be unloaded, I said to my husband, "There are those worldly goods we were talking about."

There are five of us now, but our increased possessions seem disproportionate to our population growth. Nothing brings this home more than unpacking and putting away the accumulation of nearly three decades of marriage, family, and travel.

The frequent moves of military life keep us well acquainted with the extent of our acquisitions.

We unpack every box every time, forcing ourselves to face the stockpile, to re-evaluate what we have and why we still have it. It's a blessing and curse of military life that I have to wonder whether I should keep every precious kindergarten drawing, maps of cities we've visited, programs from school plays, and many more items of no value beyond sentimental. If we didn't transport them so often, I'd save them without question; the downside is that I might end up on one of those housecleaning intervention shows on TV.

"Mom, do you want to keep this?" I look up from unpacking a box of dishes to see what my youngest is holding. A nametag sticker my husband wore when we took our oldest son to college orientation his freshman year two years ago.

Well, my husband never actually wore it. I wrote his name on it, but it ended up in my purse rather than on his lapel. It traveled back home to Germany with us after we left our son in Texas. I put it in his room—full of his things, but empty of him. I couldn't throw it away then. It returned to the States on this move and turned up on the floor during unpacking. A piece of my life to look at and evaluate: trash or treasure?

"So, can I throw it away?" my son asks, tired of waiting while I deliberate the fate of this tiny scrap of the past.

"Yes," I answer. It's not like I'm going to forget that day without the nametag. The same could be said of most souvenirs, but I'm a tactile person. Also, I don't trust my aging brain as the sole repository of our family history.

If we did not have to watch strangers box up our possessions every few years, if we did not later unpack it all piece by piece, if we did not have to know, by the crate and to the pound, exactly how much furniture, clothing, linens, pots, pans, and kitsch we use to re-create our family nest, would we need to evaluate everything we save?

Before every move, we clean out. We weed out. We give away. We throw away. After unpacking, we do it all again. A pile of boxes and bags by our new front door awaits the donation truck, mostly clothing, kitchenware, and small appliances. The practical stuff I can evaluate objectively. It's the sentimental stuff I can't seem to let go.

We have dozens of photo albums and scrapbooks and the materials to create more. Other items can't be confined to a page: clay creations made by little hands, board books imprinted by baby teeth. Moving makes me wonder why I save them.

Maybe someday we'll have an attic, a museum for these remnants of our family history, where they can gather dust, not inventory stickers. Maybe my grown children and grandchildren will wander through the tangible remains of their childhood, saying, "Remember that day?" "Oh, this was a great costume," or "Look, this was my favorite book!"

Until then, I guess we'll keep them as a traveling exhibit, one we revisit with every move. What could be more fitting for a military family?

★ ★ ★

Taking Inventory

January 17, 2012

I found it while cleaning house last week. I moved the kitchen trash bin to vacuum in the corner, and there it was: a little blue sticker. It was imprinted only with a number, "120," but I recognized it immediately. You would, too, because you've seen thousands like it in a rainbow of colors: an inventory sticker.

We moved here six months ago. The boxes are long since unpacked, so why did it show up now? Maybe it was on a box of Christmas decorations, recently put away. I have cleaned my floors since then. Perhaps it turned up on a sneaker sole and then was tossed in the general direction of the garbage.

One way or another, it ended up on the floor, a reminder that moving is not just something my family does every two or three years, it sticks to us all the time. The evidence is always there, hidden on the back of a dresser or in plain sight on the kitchen floor.

I shared a photo of my misplaced inventory sticker on Facebook. Several military spouse friends quickly commented:

"Oh, no! You lost part of your family history off the back of your couch! Put it back! Put it back!" said Army wife Carol Simpson.

June Herring, whose husband retired from the Air Force a few years ago, kept some of her inventory stickers on purpose.

"I still have a few that I just leave there for a good memory whenever I run across them," she said.

My mom said some of her furniture still has stickers from moves that happened decades ago. "They never all go away!" she said.

Deb Hammer, an Army wife living overseas said, "This is a reminder: Don't get too comfy 'cause eventually someone tags your things and takes them away.

"Just the other day, I was at a friend's house … admiring her very nice dining room set. I look down and see an orange sticker like this, and then I smiled because a civilian person would never understand about the sticker collections that military families have."

I'm glad I'm not the only one who gets sentimental—even philosophical—about a little bit of adhesive tape.

Our sticker collections hint at our past and future transitions. Those moves also shape the way I live in the present, honing some skills and dulling others.

For example, I'm good at moving in. Within a week or two, I can unpack the boxes, hang enough curtains and pictures to be ready for weekend guests, a birthday celebration, or even Christmas. I've done it. So have you.

I'm not so good at spring cleaning. Let me rephrase that: I don't do spring cleaning, as a general rule. I usually wait until it's moving time to de-clutter shelves and drawers, clean out closets, and deep clean under the appliances.

I'm good at making friends quickly, and just as quickly evaluating those who will remain acquaintances. I don't measure the depth of friendship by the number of hours spent together or the number of miles that separate us. My closest friends are often from military families because we don't have to explain these things to each other.

I'm not so good at saying goodbye, in spite of having plenty of practice. I'm much better at saying, "I hope our paths cross again," or "See you again soon." In military life, it is often true, by chance or by design.

Moving affects my choices, major and minor, from friendships to household furnishings. I don't buy expensive curtains. They might not fit the next house. I choose sturdy furniture so it will survive to see the next house.

Most importantly, moving affects my children. They can't name just one hometown, but they can make friends and be at home wherever they go. They may not know exactly where they are from, but they know where they've been.

One little blue inventory sticker: A reminder of the places military life takes us, the ways it changes us, and the adventures yet to come.

Those stickers are like my kids' stuffed animals. They mate and multiply overnight. Just when you think you have found them all, another one shows up. Then you get orders, and the process begins again. —Beverly Pitts

~

Those inventory stickers are little badges of honor!
—Therese Gamble

~

This [column] had me laughing and responding out loud because it is SO true!

I don't spring clean because a move is always around the corner, meaning I will be sorting and organizing and donating and throwing out ...

My civilian friends and family don't get it, but my military friends, who are scattered around the globe, definitely do. My kids have experienced so many amazing places, and don't find that extraordinary. They have no hometown, but consider the United States home. So, yep, every time I find one of our hidden stickers, I smile, knowing what it represents.

—Erin Thompson

~

We moved last summer and we move again this summer in 2012 ... I loved reading this to my daughters today as well. You are good company to have when the chaos of military life unfolds! And we have so many of those stickers on our belongings, it's kind of ridiculous! —Celeste McVeigh

~

Terri, I am going to miss those many colored stickers that seem to pop up out of nowhere. I always wonder, "What move was that color?" I may just have to leave a few on with my final move. —Jean Van Sickle

~

For more than thirty-five years, we have been "collecting stickers" from twenty-five moves thus far, so your column truly hit a chord with me. But, even better than that, it gave me something to slip in with the loaf of banana bread that greets each new neighbor, or the chicken salad sandwiches that feed movers as each old friend slips from the block. A copy of your column that speaks so tenderly to the nomadic yet endearing lifestyle that is our own will now be included from me at each of those occasions. It says it all for me, to them, as they come and go from my life.

A tiny little sticker that can tell huge stories again and again. Who'd have thought? —Christi M. Ham

★ ★ ★

Earning Our Wings

March 29, 2011

T.S. Eliot wrote, "I have measured out my life with coffee spoons." I drink my share of coffee, but if I were to measure my life as a military wife, it could easily be in trips to the airport.

I just got back from one this morning, the good kind. My husband returned from a short TDY in the States. He flew all night, getting only the quality and quantity of sleep allowed by the close proximity of strangers and the parsimonious degree of recline allowed in an airplane seat.

He's taking a midday nap now, acclimating to our time zone here in Germany, while I'm contemplating the chapters of military life bookmarked by airport visits. Sometimes I'm the one holding the ticket—mentally reviewing my packing list and connecting flights. Sometimes I'm the shuttle driver, picking up and rejoicing, or dropping off and feeling forlorn.

The best trips to the airport are those that reunite, of course, like my husband's homecoming today. The hardest ones separate: taking leave of good friends at a well-loved assignment or traveling home for my father's funeral.

My favorite kind of trip to the airport, now that I'm the parent of a college student, is when our son arrives home on school holidays. I also enjoy picking up my mom when she comes to visit and the look on her face when she sees me. Even after spending long hours on a plane, she never looks tired, only happy.

She has the same look when I am the traveler, coming home for a visit. I've seen that look from both sides now, as a mother and child, and I understand her joy. Likewise, I dread the flip-side airport trip, when it's time to say goodbye again.

There are other airport trips we don't celebrate, but barely have time to grieve either—deployment departures. Our minds are on bags, passports, tickets, and last-minute reminders, keeping us from dwelling on the lonely and uncertain months ahead. I always think these leave-takings should be more ceremonious. Instead, they're simply busy. Before we know it, we're back in the car, our number reduced by one, wondering what just happened and whether we said "I love you" and "Be safe" enough times.

Our family has spent a lifetime of travel, moving, visiting, vacationing. In the early days, we were that family with the tired children, lugging bags of diapers, toys, and snacks to fill long hours of travel. Those journeys became much easier as the kids grew big enough to carry their own bags and welcome a nap rather than resist it.

We've spent so much time in airports that we know many by initials or by name: DFW, LAX, Narita, Schipol. We know where to find the bathrooms and Starbucks in many of them. They are part of the neighborhood of our lives.

Our kids know the airport drill. They know what is allowed in a carry-on and how to get through security efficiently: laptops out, belts off, small bottles in a baggie. They can heft a suitcase and know if it's pushing the weight limit.

Now I'm preparing for another kind of airport trip. On spring break, my daughter and I will fly to the US to visit prospective colleges.

Soon it will be time for the next step, when she'll be the only one with a ticket to ride. We'll be the shuttle crew, with last-minute questions, reminders, and tears. She'll wave goodbye and embark on a life of independent air travel. We'll get back in the car, our number again reduced by one, wondering whether we said "I love you" and "Be safe" enough times, wondering how our baby girl could be old enough to get on a plane by herself.

Another chapter measured by yet another trip to the airport.

★ ★ ★

Visiting Hometowns and Coming Home

August 24, 2008

Our family just returned from fifty days of travel in the United States. We flew thousands of miles and drove thousands more. We lived out of suitcases; ate fast food and home cooking; slept in hotels, guest rooms, and on living room floors across two continents and ten states—a vacation as nomadic as our military life.

From Independence Day with my husband's family in North Carolina to my sister's wedding day in Oklahoma, we covered a lot of territory, some new, some familiar.

We visited friends, family, and prospective colleges. Our oldest earned his driver's permit, and we all went to Disney World.

Our travels took us through places we once called home in Alabama, Georgia, and Texas. Each seemed familiar and strange at the same time.

Our transient life deepens my appreciation for home and for sweet moments spent in hometowns, some borrowed and some remembered:

July 4—Charlotte, North Carolina: Sitting in lawn chairs on a tree-lined street, we watched a red, white, and blue neighborhood parade of kids on bicycles, families pushing strollers, walking dogs, and others waving from convertibles.

An afternoon barbecue brought together the extended and blended family to enjoy the backyard pool, watermelon, and Granny's homemade potato salad.

After dark, a few fireflies and the kids' sparklers outshone the evening's fireworks.

July 9—Atlanta: We visited Georgia Tech, then had burgers, slaw dogs, and onion rings at a local institution, The Varsity Drive-In.

July 15—Montgomery, Alabama: My daughter celebrated her fifteenth birthday in a way that is becoming a reluctant tradition—in a hotel.

July 18—New Orleans: Crossed twenty-six miles of bridge over Lake Pontchartrain to ride the streetcars and enjoy the city with Nancy, best friend and tour guide extraordinaire.

Highlights included burgers and pecan pie at The Camellia Grill; the calliope on the Natchez Queen playing "Seventy-six Trombones"; beignets at Café Du Monde, jazz music on the sidewalks of the French Quarter, and spending time with Nancy.

July 28—Waco, Texas: Toured my alma mater, Baylor University, with one of my college roommates, her children plus mine. We spent that evening at an Italian restaurant with no children and two more of our roomies, breathing new life into the old days.

August 4—Altus, Oklahoma: Lattes with my mom at our favorite coffee shop. The owners have been in business on Main Street for about thirty years and keep photo albums of friends who are also customers, including Mom, my sisters, my children, and me. It's nice to go where people know my name and ask, "Where do you live now?"

August 8—Fletcher, Oklahoma: Sat with my grandmother at her kitchen table, looking at old pictures and talking about my grandfather, while my youngest son explored the basement, a favorite pastime of mine when I was his age.

August 11—Tuttle, Oklahoma: My dad gave my oldest son a driving lesson in Dad's '69 Ford truck, already a classic in 1980 when I learned to drive in it.

August 16—Oklahoma City: Baby sister gets married. She was the flower girl at my wedding twenty-three years ago—almost to the day. All my sisters and all our combined ten children were in one place at one time for the first time.

Do you ever feel like your family is from everywhere, and yet from nowhere? I do. But when our travels are over and we drag our suitcases over our own threshold—whether in Georgia or Germany—we know we're home. And we're glad to be here.

★ ★ ★

Lego Blocks and Loose Screws

August 23, 2013

It's the same after every move. When our belongings are wrapped, boxed, taped and loaded on the truck, some little things get left behind. Neglected bits and pieces of our family life nestled against baseboards or hiding in corners: pennies, paperclips, odd screws. I wonder how many screws you can lose before everything starts coming apart. We must be close to our limit after a dozen moves or so. We keep a collection of loose screws, a byproduct of military life or a metaphor? Someday we might discover where they belong.

In every single move since the advent of children in our household, the post-packing detritus always includes one Lego block. Always.

Two of our children are now past twenty. Our youngest is halfway through high school. The Lego days are about over. A few months ago, as I looked around our latest empty house in Virginia, I thought, "Probably won't be any leftover Lego this time." It was sad somehow, the passing of this minute milestone of moving.

People who don't move around like we do say things like, "I guess your family is used to moving."

I suppose we are accustomed to the idea of moving. We know that each place will be our home temporarily, but I'm not sure it's possible to get used to relocating a family, even with practice. Maybe if all moves were alike, but they never are.

One move is singular, but its components are legion. Preparations, events, paperwork, goodbyes all have different impact on different family members.

There's the sadness when a first grader leaves his best friend, the panic of misplaced passports, or the terrible sound when a box of china falls from the moving truck and lands on the driveway. There are positive variables, too, like moving to an exciting location, or one that's near family or friends, leaving an ill-fitting school or job, none of which affects all family members in the same way.

For some reason, I thought the stresses of moving would diminish as our children grow and become more independent. But everyone is still jostled when home changes addresses, even those who don't live there all the time.

Spring and summer were packed with transitions and travel for our family. I'll skip the detailed itinerary and sum up: In shifting combinations of our five family members, we traveled from Virginia to Texas, back to Virginia, to Illinois, to Oklahoma, back to Texas, then back to Illinois, to California, one more time to Virginia and finally back to Illinois again—oh, and there was also TDY, too.

Every part of the journey served a purpose. At various locations we picked up, collectively, a college diploma, a new driver's license, a used car, four new tires, three new jobs, and another house to call home for a few years. Along the way, we also deposited a son in Texas, a daughter in California, and the remaining three of us in Illinois.

The usual milestones of family life become more complicated when they occur in a moving season. Seems like I should have known that.

Our daughter got her driver's license in Texas, where we're residents. She explained to the examiner that although she attends college in California, she was visiting her grandmother in Oklahoma, and taking summer classes while her parents were in transit from Virginia to Illinois.

We've all been together at least once, so for that we're thankful. We've all been to our new house, just not at the same time. For that, we look forward to the holidays.

Our youngest son started his new high school last week. After the first day, someone asked him how he liked the school and how he felt about the move.

He smiled and said he thought the school would be okay, but moving is always hard.

Yes, it is. Every move is different, but that part doesn't change. It's hard.

After the movers emptied the house in Virginia and I be-gan cleaning, I did find a Lego block after all, a tiny gray one wedged between wall and carpet. Right beside another loose screw.

★ ★ ★

Duty Calls:
Service and Sacrifice

Things That Don't Change

September 14, 2010

A page from my journal:

I watch my children waiting at the end of the driveway in their new school clothes, carrying matching backpacks and lunch boxes. They are talking and laughing together. A big yellow school bus pulls up, lights flashing and sun glinting off the windows.

The kids give me a last wave and climb up. The bus driver also waves to me, and I wonder if she envies me, standing on my porch in my jammies, a cup of coffee in hand as she drives away with forty kids in tow. "She should," I think, as I walk back into the kitchen for a refill ... then I head for our study.

One wall is lined with books, and a wingback chair is by the window. I sink into it with a sigh of contentment. My youngest is still upstairs snoozing, at least for a little while. This is the most peaceful time of the whole day.

I used to dream about having a room and chair exactly like this, a life exactly like this.

I enjoy these blessings, but I remember every day that they are not the necessities of life. Our family has been content in less idyllic circumstances. Life is full of change. Life is change. We will get a new assignment in a couple of years. The kids will grow up. Next year, all three will get on that big yellow bus ...

I ended the entry by writing a prayer, as I sometimes do:

Lord, even when the circumstances of my life seem too good to be true, help me to look only to you. I know that my joy doesn't come from these things, but from the hope I have in you ... Your ways are higher than my ways, as high as the heavens are above the earth.

When I closed my journal, it was about eight o'clock on a sunny Tuesday morning—September 11, 2001.

I didn't see the news until later. After watching television footage of smoke rising from the Pentagon, the Flight 93 crash site, and images of the Twin Towers falling over and over, I had to get outside.

Standing in my front yard, I looked up at the perfectly clear blue sky and wondered how it could remain so beautiful. Birds were still singing. Didn't they know our world had been terribly changed?

My children are all teenagers now. They don't remember much about life before that bright and sunny, but terrible Tuesday, when terrorism, war, and deployment became household words for us.

What should we remember nine years later? We'll remember the thousands who died that day and the thousands of US military men and women who have sacrificed their lives since then. As a country, even as military families, we can't help but wonder whether their sacrifices can bring another kind of change to the world. We hope and pray.

I will remember how circumstances changed in an instant—while some things, like the sky, remained the same. In news footage, huge billows of smoke from the shattered World Trade Center show up against a backdrop of intense azure, sometimes obscuring but not changing it.

As I write today, it's another beautiful September morning. Birds are singing. The sky is a clear, beautiful blue. It's a good day to remember things that cannot change.

Your ways are higher than my ways, as high as the heavens are above the earth.

★   ★   ★

Green Bags

It's September, and my husband is packing again. This month seems to coincide often with deployments. It's almost part of the back-to-school ritual: Time to get crayons, composition books, and three new sets of desert camouflage.

For many reasons, our nation pauses for reflection when the eleventh day of the ninth month approaches. I've been thinking about the strength of military families in uncertain times, and remembering other Septembers:

2001: Dark green mobility bags, zippered mouths gaping open, mar the order of our living room floor and our lives. In more peaceful days, the bags were forgotten, stacked on top of some boxes in our garage. Now they're spread out on the living room floor, demanding our attention, like the news footage from New York, Virginia, and Pennsylvania.

My husband empties the bags, scrutinizes their contents: t-shirts, camouflage gear, gas mask, first aid kit, and other necessities strewn on the carpet. One bag has a small American flag attached, at least barely. It clings by one corner, a reminder of another war, stapled to the canvas at the last minute. That was more than ten years ago. This time I'll sew it on.

In the relative peace of those years, it was easy to forget what is again clear to us. Life is uncertain.

Our children troop downstairs for breakfast and stop short when they see the bags. "Where's Daddy going?" they ask. Television scenes of fallen skyscrapers and airplanes were too distant to change their lives. The sight of Daddy's bags brings events home. We can't answer all their questions. We don't know the "when" or the "where." We can only tell them that life is uncertain, but God is not.

2005: Dark green mobility bags, zipped up and piled on the luggage cart, signal another September departure. The flag is still flying on one bag. I'm glad I sewed it on. This will be its fourth trip to another, less peaceful part of the world.

On the way to the airport, we take two of our children for their first day of school. Our eight-year-old stays with me. By the time all the goodbyes are said, and we finally drive away from the terminal, I feel numb. In the back seat, our youngest is quiet for a while, and then asks again what we've already answered: "How long will Dad be gone?"

He takes in my answer and pauses. "He'll be gone for my birthday."

"Yes, baby."

In the rearview mirror, I see he is holding back tears—four lanes of traffic and no place to pull over. Words are so useless. I want to hold him and cry with him. We've been through this before, but it doesn't get easier. When finally, I can stop the car and open his door, I tell the truth: "I need a hug." He gives it gladly, and is already chatting about our plans for the day. I've learned that sorrow comes and goes. When it comes, cry about it, and when it goes, don't call it back.

2007: A small flag still waves on one green bag as we prepare for another trip to the airport, another departure, more uncertainty. But really, the uncertainties of life are always there, relegated to the pile in the garage like the green bags used to be. Sometimes it's good to bring them into the rooms where we live, examine the contents, pack them up, and face the unknown.

Life is still uncertain, and still, God is not. I don't know any more comforting words for Septembers like these.

★　★　★

Homecomings: The Nitty Gritty

August 3, 2008

The aftermath of deployment is laundry—lots of laundry—some of it infused with sand so fine I can't see it. But I can feel it. Even weeks later, I find grit in unexpected places, a patch on the floor, between the pages of a book.

When my husband first came back from deployment in the spring, people would say, "You must be glad to have your husband back." How right they are! He is safely home, and I am thankful.

Veterans of deployment, reunion—and sand—would ask more pointedly, "How are you adjusting?" They know the nitty gritty, the friction that takes time and patience to wash away.

The transition back to family life after deployment can last as long as the deployment. It is hard work getting rid of all that irritating sand. The months of putting our lives back together are as much a test of our love and commitment as the months of absence.

After deployment a few years ago, a friend asked, "What's the biggest difference now that Mark is back?" She caught me on one of those high-friction days, and I responded unguardedly: "I can't do whatever I want to do whenever I want to do it."

At the time, our three children were six, nine, and twelve, and, truthfully, I had not been able to do "whatever I want to do whenever I want to do it" since 1990. The adjustment after deployment meant dividing my days between five people's needs instead of four.

Another friend confided that life was simpler during her husband's deployment. His absence, she said, means "one less person to please" when making daily decisions about meals and movies.

Such small things, but so are grains of sand in your swimsuit. Even small irritations can ruin your day at the beach—and make you walk funny. Ignoring them won't stop the chafing. Even the small adjustments have to be faced.

During deployment, our family spent several months compensating for the absence of an essential member. It also takes time to get used to having him back. He is here in the flesh, no longer just a voice on the phone or a recurring name in our inbox.

Absence does make the heart grow fonder, but the reverse can also be true. When we are daily rubbing elbows in the messiness of family life, fondness takes a little more work.

I admit it is sometimes easier to remember what a wonderful guy my husband truly is when he is serving his country on a foreign field and taking care of his own dirty laundry.

Likewise, care packages from home are probably more pleasant to him than snotty noses and sibling rivalry. Starting the day with a sweet email from me when he's in the desert is surely more endearing than my morning breath from the next pillow.

One wise Air Force wife puts these small irritations in perspective. "I don't mind his snoring," she said. "It means he's safe at home."

There are big things to take care of, too, after a deployment. Combat stress is a possibility. Unresolved family issues packed away upon departure will be there on arrival, falling out of the luggage along with the sandy uniforms.

It would be nice to finish up with some good advice: "Five Easy Steps to a Smooth Post-Deployment Transition." I'll leave that to public service announcements on American Forces Network. The truth is, there will be a lot more than five steps, not all of them easy. Putting a family back together takes time, patience, and love. There's a lot of laundry to do.

★ ★ ★

Telling Stories

February 28, 2011

Kristin Henderson has seen the war from the front and the home front. As a reporter, she covered troops in Iraq and Afghanistan for *The Washington Post Magazine*. As a military chaplain's wife, she's been the one at home during several deployments. Her book, *While They're at War*, tells the stories of military wives enduring deployments early in the war.

"Compared to other reporters, I've only embedded twice. I'm really a dilettante," she demurred. Compared to most spouses, though, perhaps her perspective on our decade of conflict is wider.

Relating stories that come from both fronts is Kristin's passion as a writer and a military wife, so she listens.

"I've never heard a boring story from anybody ... There is always something interesting there if you are just willing to sit and listen," Kristin said.

"People just want to be heard, to know they aren't forgotten, and that what they do is recognized and respected."

Conditions were primitive and reporters were scarce in 2008 when she embedded with a Marine unit in Helmand province. "Everyone was in Iraq," she said, so she went to Afghanistan.

"I really was there to tell the story of that particular platoon. The Marines were talking about how glad they were that USAID was there because they couldn't do it alone."

It was a chance for Kristin to hear directly from the troops what they were discovering about how the war could be won—not only with bullets, but also with humanitarian aid.

"I showed up at this outpost where there had been no women," she said. "They were living in a school that had a tarp for a roof, with classrooms as dorm rooms. I had a dorm room all to myself ... I had a cot, and they had put down some plywood on the dirt. Quite the swank accommodations, considering where we were."

One night, she hiked up a dark mountain with a group of

Marines, delivering supplies to men at a remote observation post.

"For about three days at a time, five guys would be holed up on this mountain," she said. "It was freezing cold up there."

"As I was leaving, one guy grabbed me by the elbow and said, 'Ma'am, I just want to thank you for coming all the way out here. Not many people would do that just to see what we do.'"

His gratitude stunned her.

"I think at that time, they felt so alone and forgotten by the rest of the country. There was no media there. No one was telling their story."

Troops on dark mountaintops and spouses struggling at home want to know their sacrifice has value, that their story has listeners.

"Interest in military families comes in little flurries, like interest in the war," Kristin said. "It's all off the front page now. Most people want to be supportive … but they don't know what to do but give you a pat on the back.

"While sympathy and admiration on the civilian side has grown, the experience of being at war has outpaced that," she said. "Most of our service members are changed when they come home. You and I are changed, families are changed, and it gets compounded with every deployment."

In almost ten years of war, Kristin has seen advances in the way the military cares for its own.

"I think there have been huge improvements in military culture and the systems they have in place," she said, particularly for handling combat stress.

"Even as the system changes, the reality is that one individual who is unenlightened can bring it all to a screeching halt. For the subordinates under their command, life is no different than it was before.

"Yes, there are vast improvements, but we still have a ways to go," Kristin said. "As long as there are some leaders who still see the need to process stress experiences as a weakness, that stigma is going to remain in individual cases."

People inside and outside the military are questioning whether the price paid by military families during these years of war has been worthwhile, she said.

"I think the argument can be made that much has been accomplished, in spite of not being given the resources to fight the right kind of battle," she said.

To answer the question "Has it been worthwhile?" Kristin takes her answer to the individual level.

"For me, what makes life meaningful is leaving the world a slightly better place than you found it. Following all the larger news, it's easy to feel helpless to change anything because the problems are so large, much larger than any one person, even the president of the United States," she said.

"When I look at the larger issue of 'Is the military being used well?' it can be very discouraging, but when I look at the individual level, and I look at what my husband does, I know he's helping people on a day-to-day basis and making a difference. That makes it worthwhile to me."

And so she keeps telling the stories.

★ ★ ★

Gary and Lt. Dan

September 25, 2012

Being stuck in traffic between his charity work and his day job might be a metaphor for the life of Gary Sinise. The actor plays Detective Mac Taylor on "CSI: NY." He's possibly better known in military circles for another character with the same last name, Lt. Dan Taylor of *Forrest Gump*, and for his work on behalf of wounded veterans.

After an event in Temecula, California, where his Gary Sinise Foundation helped provide a house for a wounded Marine, the actor was on his way to the Los Angeles studio where he is shooting season nine of *CSI: NY.*

"I'm trying to get back to work right now, and the traffic is preventing me," Sinise said.

LA's gridlock worked in my favor, because Sinise used the travel delay to talk to me by phone about his efforts for American troops.

"This morning, we presented the keys to Marine Cpl. Juan Dominguez, who lost both legs and an arm, and obviously has some special needs, so we built a specially-designed home just for him," Sinise said. "We had a great ceremony right out in front of his house."

Sinise's foundation, alongside the Stephen Siller Tunnel to Towers Foundation, is building specially designed homes for veterans returning from war with life-altering injuries. The program, called Building for America's Bravest, gets fundraising and publicity power from the Lt. Dan Band, named for the double-amputee Vietnam veteran Sinise portrayed.

The Lt. Dan Band, with Sinise on bass guitar, performs forty or fifty shows yearly all over the world, at military installations, hospitals, USO events, or fundraisers, like those that help fund the homes for veterans.

Sinise usually spends weekdays in California with his family and at work on the *CSI* set. The band's schedule keeps him on the road most weekends—eleven months of the year.

"I usually try to take January off," said Sinise. This year, however, there was a January gig in Kuwait he didn't want to miss.

"I was on the very first USO tour over there in June of 2003," he said. "This was going to be the last entertainment tour for troops who have served in Iraq, so I couldn't pass that up ... I took the band over and we played a concert in Kuwait."

Sinise began touring for the USO at the outset of the war in Afghanistan and formed the Lt. Dan Band in 2003. His objectives soon moved beyond entertainment. Nearly a decade later, the band has become a vehicle for raising money and awareness for veteran and military issues.

Their touring schedule includes many military locations and small communities. Fundraisers for Building for America's Bravest usually happen in towns where the houses will be, to make the community aware of the veteran.

"That person is going to need community support," Sinise said. "We can build houses, but I think it's important for the community to rally around these wounded warriors who have given so much of themselves."

On another front, Sinise has created public service announcements for the US Marine Corps suicide prevention resource, called "DStress Line."

"It might help to see that there are Americans out there who didn't serve, which I didn't, who just believe in helping and supporting our military," he said.

He's not a veteran, but Sinise's connections to the military are many. He serves on the council of the Congressional Medal of Honor Foundation, for example. He said getting to know Medal of Honor recipients motivates him to do what he does.

"They inspire me ... to go out and continue to do what I know I'm capable of doing. I always tell folks, if you can think it, you can do it. If you're capable of doing something to serve, then I think you should, and when you do, you get a lot out of it yourself."

After learning the schedule he keeps and the scope of his philanthropic work, only partially covered here, I wanted to ask Sinise if he considers himself driven, but there wasn't time. He had more phone interviews to complete during the traffic jam.

Which pretty much answered my question. Thanks, Lt. Dan.

★ ★ ★

A Measure of Sisterhood

March 15, 2011

She's a working mother of four who has moved many times during her twenty-two-year marriage. Her husband's career takes him away from home, often overseas and on short notice. Lee Woodruff is not a military wife, but she could claim a measure of sisterhood.

Her initiation came at a place no one chooses, the bedside of her injured husband at Landstuhl Regional Medical Center in Germany.

Bob Woodruff, then an anchor for *ABC News*, suffered a traumatic brain injury (TBI), caused by a roadside bomb in 2006, while traveling with an Army unit in Iraq.

"Bob was not a warrior, but he was a firm believer that as long as there were Americans putting their lives on the line for us, there needed to be journalists telling their story," said Lee. "He was serving his country in a different way."

The Woodruffs encountered military families with wounded loved ones at Landstuhl and later the National Naval Medical Center at Bethesda, Maryland, where Bob also was treated.

"Bob had gotten so much attention as a news anchor," she said. "Yet this was happening to families around the country every day, and nobody was really aware of it."

Lee recalled one of Bob's doctors telling her, "You're a writer, and you should write a book about this experience. Nobody out there in America knows that there are thousands of young men and women in these hospitals with these kinds of injuries."

Since then, Lee has written two books. The first, *In an Instant*, cowritten with Bob in 2007, chronicles their individual paths through his injury and the early days of his recovery.

Her second book, *Perfectly Imperfect: A Life in Progress*, grew out of the first. Both began during the five weeks her husband lay in a coma.

"Everybody at the hospital tells you just to talk, because that's knitting his brain back together," Lee said. "So I would just tell him the stories of our life."

Telling became writing, as Lee tried to make sense of the tragedy through her craft.

Not all the stories fit in the first book, and Lee wanted to share the remainder. *Perfectly Imperfect* is a series of essays, stories that connect women as wives, parents, sisters, and daughters.

"They are two different books, but the connection is always there of the big bad thing, that moment in life when you hit the gritty part of the pavement that we're probably all going to meet at some point in one form or another."

The nitty-gritty events described in *Perfectly Imperfect* include miscarriage, aging parents, aging self, parenting teens, Bob's injury, recovery, and Lee's experiences as a caregiver.

"There are a lot of caregivers who wonder why they feel so sad after the worst is over," she said.

Right after the injury, Lee said she felt the need to be positive for her kids and push worst-case scenarios to the back of her mind.

"I had a lot of hope, especially when Bob woke up. The healing took place at such a rapid pace," she said. "I'd walk into that hospital each day and see something new."

But there's no escaping the changes that TBI brings to a family.

"Reality can set in even a year or two later," she said, bringing sadness and even depression. It's all part of what Lee calls "the backlash of the dragon's tail" for caregivers.

"You stay up for so long, and, ultimately, what goes up must come down. You don't have the opportunity when you are in the middle of the fire to grieve or be angry or go through those normal cycles."

She said faith, family, and friends got her through dark days and gave her hope.

"I think I leaned on those three pillars in different measures at different times, depending on the day."

Lee's sense of humor, evident in her writing and conversation, was another source of strength.

"It lets the air out, in some ways, so that you can stay sane," she said. "When you are laughing from your diaphragm, it's impossible to cry. Laughter feels normal, and laughter connects people."

Recovery from brain injury is a long haul, Lee cautioned.

"It's certainly not a broken leg," she said, though she describes Bob's recovery as "miraculous."

He has returned to work as a correspondent for *ABC News* and, more importantly, to his family.

In 2008, the Woodruffs started the Bob Woodruff Foundation to raise awareness of hidden injuries like TBI, PTSD, and combat-stress related issues. The foundation has raised $11 million, which it invests in education and awareness about TBI and reintegration programs for veterans with all kinds of injuries.

Lee said they wanted to find something positive in their experience to show their children that good things can come out of bad. The foundation aims to get Americans involved, engaged, and aware of the price paid by military families.

"Bob felt a real affinity and still does with the military," Lee said. "We both felt this was the right thing to do.

"Nobody comes back from a brain injury 100 percent," she said. "I'm so thrilled for where Bob is, but I still grieve the little things that other people may not see. That doesn't minimize what families go through whose loved ones have more severe consequences.

"When he goes to visit soldiers in the hospital and sees people who are less well off than he is, he comes back profoundly quiet ... It's very sobering. We are so lucky, I'm not sure why.

"We are one couple in our own little corner trying to do something with our outcome that will hopefully make it better for everyone," said Lee.

"That's all we can do."

★ ★ ★

Rolling Out the Red Carpet

November 15, 2011

A makeshift fashion salon came alive in a Manhattan hotel conference room. A-list stylists selected evening dresses from laden racks, sizing their clients at a glance. Others offering footwear carried bouquets of stilettos by the heels. Sparkly jewelry was doled out like candy. Professional photographers crisscrossed the room, capturing the results of the stylists' handiwork.

"One more, please. Everybody look this way."

The women being attired were not models, but the photos showed they could be. Not celebrities, but maybe they should be. The purpose of this fashion confab was to style and pamper fifty caregivers of wounded veterans, preparing them for a red carpet walk at a celebrity fundraiser.

Most are wives; some are mothers or sisters. A few are wounded veterans. All are women whose lives were changed by the injuries of war.

The wounded veterans and their loved ones were guests of honor at Stand Up For Heroes, a New York fundraising event for the Bob Woodruff Foundation. The foundation raises money for organizations that help injured troops and their families.

Caregivers—mostly women—don't always have much time to focus on their wardrobes, said Anne Marie Dougherty, Marine wife and marketing and communications director for the foundation.

So the foundation created a beauty fest for the women before the event: Day one for head-to-toe wardrobe, day two for hair and makeup.

New York stylist Mary Alice Stephenson said she called her "best girlfriends," including Lucy Sykes Rellie and Ann Caruso, to give military family members the celebrity treatment.

Mary Alice and friends—whose clients are known by first names like Beyonce, Scarlett, and Brittany—brought a cadre of other stylists. Also taking part was a design team from Sears, whose corporation donated all the clothing, shoes, and accessories the women received.

L'Oreal and Dior professionals came on board for makeup and hair.

The women were welcomed as they entered the fashion zone and ushered to the racks of dresses to begin the process.

"I wear an eight or a ten," said Sunny, an Army wife.

"Oh, no you don't," asserted a pert stylist with an asymmetrical haircut. "Ma-aybe a six, probably a four." She was right.

Particular attention was paid to the shoes for another young woman—one was for her prosthesis. She chose shimmery flats with rhinestones to match the ones on her purple chiffon dress.

Dresses were pinned, custom fitted, and delivered the next day.

A discreetly placed table offered foundation garments and stockings.

"Woo hoo, girl!" said Mary Alice, breaking off mid-conversation with a reporter. She had noticed a woman emerging shyly from a fitting room in a form-flattering gown. "You look spectacular!"

Laughter drifted into the hallway from the wide-open doors. Military wives mingled with fashion mavens, a few famous faces, and the occasional TV crew. No nametags or signs identified donors for the cameras. No executives schmoozed with the media.

Veterans, some in wheelchairs, others with prosthetics and service dogs, some with less apparent wounds, walked the halls. They greeted friends, admired their wives' new dresses and smiled for cameras.

It was a day for smiles and almost no tears. Almost.

April came from Georgia to be there with her husband. He was recently informed of his discharge from the Air Force after fifteen years, she said, while waiting for her fashion appointment.

"It just came in the mail. No 'Thank you for your service,' just, 'You have until this date to out-process,'" she said.

Her voice broke when she said they'd depleted her retirement savings for living expenses after his injury.

"I hate to hear that story," a man sitting nearby said after April left. "The Army really took care of us after I was injured."

Soon his wife came out, holding her garment bag of red carpet elegance.

Gloria, another caregiver, demonstrated her catwalk stride in a red dress and strappy high heels. But diva turned mom seconds later, giving instructions to another relative who offered to take her son outside in his wheelchair.

"Be sure he has his hat on," she said, pulling a jacket around her son's shoulders.

"The best part is seeing my husband in his uniform," said Ernestine. The veterans are encouraged to wear their uniforms to the Stand Up For Heroes concert.

"I thought he wouldn't want to wear it, but he was excited about it," she said of her husband, who walks on two prosthetic legs.

In another conference room at the same hotel, a very different event unfolded behind closed doors. Representatives of a professional sports association populated by millionaires haggled over player contracts. ESPN camped outside, and large men in expensive suits rebuffed uninvited reporters.

But the real stars scarcely noticed. They were living it up right next door, hamming for the cameras, laughing in the face of hardship, celebrating life and real heroes.

★ ★ ★

Operation Homecoming: Stories to Tell

September 14, 2008

"These troops, to me, are not just stenographers, mechanically recording their experiences. They have created and crafted real literature, and like all great works of art, they have transcended the subject matter. They are not just about war. They are about despair, grief, hope, resilience; all these emotions that civilians and military alike can empathize, understand, and learn from."

—*Andrew Carroll*

~

The gathering at the post library in Germany was small but significant: a few active duty personnel, some patients and medical staff from Landstuhl Regional Medical Center, a handful of librarians, a retiree or two, and at least one military spouse.

They came to hear about "Operation Homecoming: Writing the Wartime Experience," a National Endowment for the Arts initiative that encourages military members and families to put their experiences on paper.

"Nobody writes with greater authenticity or authority than those who've experienced themselves the hardships of war," Andrew Carroll, author of the bestseller, *Letters of a Nation*, told the group.

Thousands of pages of stories, songs, poems, and other works have been submitted since the initiative began in 2004, said Carroll. He is visiting military installations across Germany, emphasizing the importance of writing and preserving these stories.

Carroll and a diverse group of American writers, including Tom Clancy, Bobbie Ann Mason, and James McBride, have conducted writing workshops around the world for military members.

Some of the writing was compiled into a book, *Operation Homecoming*, which Carroll edited. A companion documentary was nominated this year for an Academy Award and several Emmys.

"These writings contain a great amount of heartbreak, pain, and suffering," Carroll said. "It's important that we hear them, because one of the greatest disservices we can do to those who serve and to their families is to romanticize or sanitize in any way these experiences."

Although writing can be healing, Carroll said the primary mission of Operation Homecoming is not therapy, but history, preserving firsthand accounts from troops and family members.

"From the very beginning, the NEA included the homefront: the children, the spouses, the parents," Carroll said. "This is a part of the war experience, and they, too, serve, as you all well know."

After Carroll's presentation, including readings from the book and documentary excerpts, the listeners stayed around for coffee, questions, and conversation.

Carroll shook hands with a woman who apologized for arriving late. She was in uniform, having evidently come straight from work. Someone introduced her as a doctor at LRMC, and Carroll thanked her for her service.

"It's really an honor to do what we do," she said.

Some asked the author how to submit their stories to Operation Homecoming. Others sipped coffee and told their stories to each other.

"My kids want to know when I'm coming back," said an Army reservist to the woman next to her.

"How many kids do you have?"

"Twenty."

In response to elevated eyebrows, she explained, "I'm a teacher."

Back in Pittsburgh, she teaches preschool. With her military unit, she recently built a school in Central America.

"You should have seen those kids' faces when they saw that school," she said. "If they saw a library like this, they would think it was Christmas."

A new assignment brought her to Germany.

One man had just returned from two years in Iraq. He seemed to prefer watching and listening rather than talking.

Another man quietly asked Carroll for an Operation Homecoming packet to give to another soldier from his unit.

Carroll spoke to each person and encouraged several who said they might have something to write about.

Earlier in the evening, Carroll emphasized the reason to preserve these stories.

"We think of memorials and monuments constructed by stone and metal," he said. "But to me, these very ... fragile pieces of paper are a memorial to these troops and their families, because it is their voices, their words.

"No one can tell their stories better than they can."

★ ★ ★

Pages From Life
June 12, 2008

Natalie was not happy when her dad was in Iraq for a year, but she is pretty excited about seeing her deployment experiences in a new picture book for children, according to her grandmother, who wrote the book.

In the book and in real life, Natalie calls her grandparents Papa and Nana, but the rest of the country knows them better as Vice President Joe Biden and his wife, Dr. Jill Biden.

Jill Biden's first book, *Don't Forget, God Bless Our Troops*, was just released. With words and illustrations, it tells the story of Natalie and her little brother, Hunter, during the 2008 deployment of their father, Beau Biden, who serves in the Army National Guard. The ways the family coped with the separation are depicted in the pages of the book and even the words of the title, spoken by Natalie.

"She loves the book," said Dr. Biden of Natalie's reaction. "I keep telling her what a great thing she has done, because other children will learn what it's like and other children will benefit from her book."

Natalie and Hunter may participate in some readings or other book events with their grandmother.

"I'd love to have them, because it is their story, and they're very proud of their story, and they're very proud of their dad," Dr. Biden said.

"We all have our Army shirts and every time they put theirs on, they're like, 'Nana, go get your Army shirt. Put your Army shirt on like us.' They have a real sense of pride."

Natalie's camouflage-print t-shirt is one of the real pieces of the Biden children's lives that appear in the book. Others include Natalie losing a baby tooth while her father watched via video chat, saying prayers for their father and other soldiers, and helpful neighbors who shoveled snow for the family.

"Everything that is in the book was a real occurrence, and I felt that all children, whether they were military or nonmilitary, could relate to it," said Dr. Biden.

Although the issues of deployment and family separation are serious ones, she said she wanted the book to be uplifting for children. Another purpose was to educate people of any age who don't know any military members or families.

"What better way to let Americans learn about this experience than a children's book, where the parents can read to the children, or the children might hear it in their classroom or when they go to the library," she said.

"I'm a teacher, so I thought this was a really good way to try to educate a whole generation of Americans, who have no real relationship with military families, to learn what this is all about."

In a thirty-year teaching career, Dr. Biden has taught at both the high school and college levels, and reading is one of her areas of specialization. Since moving to Washington, DC, with her husband's latest job, she has continued her career, teaching at a local community college.

Various roles in her life came together to help shape this book, she said, and to address a subject that is important to her—military families.

"I'm an educator, I'm a military mom, and now I'm second lady. I always said I wouldn't waste my platform, and I really want to do things that are meaningful. I have so many choices, but this is so close to my heart because of our son Beau."

She said she talks about military life in her own classroom and encourages others to do the same and to be aware of military children who may be in their classrooms.

"Every year (as second lady), I host the teachers of the year from every state," she said. "I talk to them about incorporating military children and awareness into their curriculum."

Dr. Biden has pledged all her earnings from the book to the USO to be used for scholarships for children of wounded and fallen servicemembers.

★ ★ ★

Invasion: Ten Years Later

March 29, 2013

Until I saw it on the news I had forgotten the date, but I remember the invasion of Iraq. The anchorman said March 20 was the tenth anniversary, but I can't remember just one day. For several days and nights in late March of 2003, I was torn between being glued to the television and avoiding it.

On almost every channel, the progress of American forces advancing toward Baghdad was covered by embedded journalists, like a horde of sports reporters giving play by play for a giant game of Risk. But it was no game. The risk was real, and my husband was over there—somewhere.

Like plenty of other military spouses, I didn't know exactly where my husband was. I couldn't reassure myself that he was away from the hostilities that were datelined Basrah, Nasiriyah, and other locations on the march northward. I knew where I thought he was—information I was not supposed to have and could not discuss with anyone—but comfort was elusive. Distance from the battles being shown on TV was no guarantee of safety. Not every dangerous place had its own reporter.

Troops were at risk every day in Afghanistan, too, in 2003, but that conflict was sparsely reported. While the Iraq invasion was still in progress, a helicopter from our base crashed into a mountain in Afghanistan. The entire crew of six was killed, all from our small community.

The day of the memorial service for the fallen crew, most of our city and county law enforcement turned out and lined the streets leading to the front gate of our base. Volunteers cared for children during the service and provided a meal at the chapel for the bereaved families afterward.

The national news barely mentioned the loss. All their big-name reporters were in Iraq, but then we didn't need news coverage to remind us there was more than one war going on. We certainly didn't care which one was getting the most press. Both were major invasions in the lives of our families.

Life on the home front plodded on as the troops moved toward Baghdad. Sick kids and soccer practice, piano lessons, work, and grocery shopping. I wrote in my journal on March 29, 2003: "It seems odd to go on with daily routines and ... life with a war going on on the other side of the world, where there are people in danger and people dying." I didn't know that daily dichotomy would continue until it felt normal.

The obligatory ten-year retrospectives of the Iraq war are predictable. Journalists and politicians are either consumed with angsty introspection about what they should have done differently or with self-righteous and thinly veiled I-told-you-sos.

Neither one does any good unless it changes the way we approach conflicts in the future. Military families don't have the luxury of analyzing why we've spent the last decade-plus at war. In some ways, it doesn't even matter which war we've spent it in. What matters is that we did spend it, and it can't be unspent.

Ten years later, what we do need is for America and its leaders to turn their thoughts to maintaining a strong and effective military as budget cuts fall in painful places. Ten years from now, what will matter is whether our government kept the promises it made to servicemen and women, and whether it cared for those who returned wounded in body and mind, and for the families of those who didn't return at all.

If our country doesn't get these things right, if it doesn't keep its promises to those who answered the call to serve this time, who will answer the call next time?

★ ★ ★

Ernie Pyle: Across Many Aprils

April 17, 2012

His was the first biography I ever read—at least the first one that had real chapters and more words than pictures. I was in the fifth grade, and I have not forgotten the story of his life, writing, and ultimately his sacrifice. His name was Ernie Pyle.

Faithful chronicler of military men on the frontlines of WWII, Pyle covered the war from the Battle of Britain, even before the US entered the war, to the D-Day invasion at Normandy, through campaigns in North Africa and Italy, to the cusp of victory in the Pacific.

His syndicated column appeared in hundreds of American newspapers, including *Stars and Stripes*. Pyle endeared himself to the fighting forces with his straightforward reporting of their lives. When he was killed near Okinawa by machine-gun fire, a hand-lettered wooden sign reflected his status among servicemen. It read: "At this spot, the 77th Infantry Division lost a buddy, Ernie Pyle, 18 April, 1945."

Pyle's work gave stateside readers a soldiers-eye view of the war. Troops on the battlefront read about themselves in his stories in *Stars and Stripes*, as the wartime editions followed the frontlines throughout WWII. The paper's staff and production physically accompanied the divisions as they fought their way forward.

The library and archive at *Stars and Stripes* headquarters in Washington, DC, holds volumes of US history recorded by the paper. The WWII papers fill several shelves. Labels on the spines of bound editions trace the advance of the Allies across Europe, from London, Marseilles, Liege, and eventually to Southern Germany. Other editions covered Northern Africa, the Mediterranean, and later, the Pacific theater.

The paper that carried Ernie Pyle's words to the troops began publication in the European theater of operations exactly three years before his death. On April 18, 1942, the paper that served troops in previous wars was drafted for duty in WWII.

That same morning, as the new *Stars and Stripes* rolled off the presses in London, Jimmy Doolittle and his Tokyo Raiders carried out the first bombing of mainland Japan. In 1945, publication of *Stars and Stripes* would arrive on the Japanese mainland as well. Both the European and Pacific editions have been in continuous publication ever since those beginnings.

The day before his death, Pyle's column in *Stars and Stripes* was about the sailors he met on board an aircraft carrier en route to what would be his final battlefield on Ie Shima, a tiny Pacific island.

"That's the way things go in wartime," he wrote, describing more than the sailors' lives. Two days later, *Stripes* carried his obituary. Pyle died with an unfinished column about victory in Europe tucked in his pocket, just four months shy of victory in the Pacific.

The late Andy Rooney, a colleague and friend of Ernie Pyle, started his journalism career as an enlisted combat reporter for *Stars and Stripes* in 1942. In an interview marking an earlier *Stripes* milestone, he predicted that the paper had run its course. From his perspective, it was a wartime paper that served a wartime purpose—to inform the troops.

"It probably should have gone out of business after the war," Rooney told a *Washington Post* writer in 1992. Then *Stripes* had only fifty years to commemorate. Now it has seventy.

"Do you think *Stars and Stripes* is on its way out?" a military friend asked me last week. Looming budget cuts have us all wondering how our lives will change. I don't claim objectivity here, but as long as there is an American military community overseas, we need an independent military newspaper that speaks to them and for them.

I never heard whether Rooney changed his mind about *Stars and Stripes*. I'd like to think he would have if he had lived side-by-side with today's military, telling their life stories, as he and his friend Ernie Pyle did for the troops seventy years ago.

★ ★ ★

Bobby's Flag

April 12, 2011

In the black and white photo, my father stands in an Oklahoma cemetery in his dress blues, arms crossed in front of him. Next to him is a solemn-faced boy cradling the triangle of a folded flag. The back of the snapshot says Bobby was eight years old when it was taken at his father's funeral in 1968.

My father was there as military escort for Bobby's father's body, returned for burial in his home state. I don't know who took the photo. I wasn't there, but I was there the day Bobby's father died.

Bob and his family lived next door to us in base housing, an Air Force family like ours. They had four sons. Bobby was the oldest, and the youngest was an infant.

I was about five, closer to the ages of Bobby's two middle brothers. As military neighbors do, Bobby's mom had been babysitting me that morning while my mom was at a doctor's appointment, and my dad was working. When she returned, my mother stayed awhile to chat over coffee. Bob was home, and my mom remembers he seemed carefree, enjoying his wife's homemade donuts.

Soon after my mom took me home, she heard sirens. Someone pounded on our door, warning us that shots had been fired in our neighborhood, telling us to lock the doors and stay low. I remember lying on the living room floor, looking up at the sun streaming through the windows, cradling our little dog as my mother cradled me.

Worse news would follow. We learned that Bob had taken his own life and the lives of his two middle sons. It must have happened shortly after we left.

After the danger was past, Mom let me play in our yard. I hid behind a tree when I saw a uniformed man walk into our house carrying an unconscious woman. I knew it was Bobby's mom, and as a child I thought she might be dead, too.

When I asked my mom about this memory, she told me the poor woman had to be sedated after seeing the bodies of her husband and two little sons. Paramedics brought her to our house to sleep so she would not be alone.

If this happened today, she might have been admitted to the hospital. In 1968, she was left with a twenty-something neighbor—my mom—and a bottle of sleeping pills.

"When she woke up, it was horrible," my mother said. "She would just hang on to me and say, 'Why, why?'"

But there was no note, no answer. What explanation would suffice? Perhaps Bob had convinced himself that his wife would be better off without him, but what quantum leap of logic led him to end his sons' brief lives?

My family and Bobby's lost touch not long after he had his photo taken with my father in that Oklahoma cemetery. I wish I knew how the remnant of his family bore up under the weight of their tragic loss. I hope they found the help and comfort their father couldn't find or didn't know how to seek.

★ ★ ★

TAPS: More Than a Sad Song

June 5, 2008

Fish splashed, geese chattered, and long-legged herons skimmed the surface of the Tidal Basin in Washington, DC, as tour buses rolled into visitors' parking at the nearby Lincoln Memorial.

White marble and limestone structures on the National Mall contrasted with red flowers, bright flags, and a blue sky. The alabaster city gleamed, undimmed and even enhanced by human tears that Sunday morning.

Two of the buses carried placards that said "Tragedy Assistance Program for Survivors: Caring for the Families of our Fallen Heroes." The passengers who disembarked had more in common than their red t-shirts. Each had lost a family member who served in the military. They came from as far away as Hawaii to remember their loved ones together.

Over Memorial Day weekend, about two thousand people participated in the Eighteenth Annual TAPS National Military Survivor Seminar. The events included a speech by Vice President Joe Biden, a Good Grief Camp for children, and this gathering at the Lincoln Memorial.

The group I encountered there had badges of honor: photo buttons of those they had lost, ribbons listing their service branch and relationship. One couple wore "parent" ribbons. A young mom with a toddler and an infant wore a "spouse" ribbon.

I read Suzie's ribbons. She had several.

"Does this mean you lost a child and your husband?" I asked.

"Yes, my husband and my son," she said, fingering the ribbons that said "parent" and "spouse." She said her teenage son had taken his own life months before his Army father died of cancer.

She wore an "Army" ribbon for her husband of twenty-seven years. Another ribbon said "Marines" for her oldest son, now serving in Afghanistan. He had called her earlier that morning, and she talked about how excited she was to hear his voice.

Laurie's ribbons said "Navy" and "sibling," and her button was a picture of her brother. A Navy reservist herself, Laurie also serves as a peer mentor for TAPS.

She and Suzie talked animatedly about those they had lost, remembering what made them laugh and what made them angry.

Being with other bereaved families is a relief, Suzie said. It's good not to have to explain, to be with people who just know and understand. TAPS events, counselors, and peer mentors are intended to provide that safe environment. The organization reaches out to anyone who has lost a loved one in military service, regardless of location or cause of death.

Providing more than a common bond, TAPS is equipped to give practical help as well, such as grief and trauma resources and information, casualty casework assistance, and crisis intervention.

"Civilians just think we're taken care of when a family loses a military member," said Laurie. Although there are programs in place—government, military, and private—for bereaved families, the support doesn't happen automatically. When families are overwhelmed by a loss, they may not know where to turn. Organizations like TAPS can help a family locate and navigate available resources.

TAPS founder Bonnie Carroll led the group to the steps of the Lincoln Memorial, where they observed a moment of silence for their loved ones and sang "God Bless America." Observers wiped away tears and took photos. The ones wearing the red shirts cheered and smiled.

Bonnie stood out from the crowd in her white t-shirt that day, but she wore a photo and ribbons like the rest. She created the organization after her Army husband was killed in a 1992 plane crash.

It was Suzie's first time to be with other grieving families since her staggering losses only months ago. She measured her progress in small steps, like being able to talk about her loss and use what she called the "S" word, suicide.

"Now I can say the words," she said. "I still feel like I'm going to throw up, but I can say the words."

One of Suzie's ribbons said simply "survivor," another S-word that she is learning to use.

★　★　★

Words of Hope

October 23, 2012

"I feel a deep sense of hopelessness," one woman wrote on the Spouse Calls blog about her husband's post-traumatic stress disorder. "Is there anyone out there living with someone with PTSD that is coping? ... I need someone to tell me if it's possible to live with someone who has this disease."

Another spouse asked, "Does it ever get better? I have faith that my husband will one day open his heart to me, but sometimes it's so hard to keep positive when I feel like I am dying inside."

These questions are hard to hear, much less answer. So when I heard about Andrea Carlile's book, *The War That Came Home*, about surviving PTSD, I called to hear her story.

Andrea said hopelessness was familiar territory for her. Her husband Wesley's post-traumatic stress destroyed their marriage and brought Andrea to contemplate suicide. She said she realized she had to live for her two young daughters, but it was a difficult journey back to wholeness for her and her family.

She said faith, therapy, compassion, and understanding were each essential to the healing they've experienced. Andrea and Wesley were separated and on their way to divorce before they were reunited.

"Our marriage was transformed over a period of the course of a year," she said, "from a horrible situation to a much healthier relationship."

Andrea said she and Wesley wanted to tell their story to give other families a reason to hope.

"I hear the same statements repeatedly," from other wives of PTSD sufferers, Andrea said. "They say: 'I thought I was alone. ... It feels good to know someone else out there has lived through this, and they were able to get through it.'"

Anne Freund, a clinical psychologist with the Department of Veterans Affairs and author of *Taming the Fire Within*, said recognition of the problem is an important step.

"The more you know about PTSD and the natural reactions to war, the better you can cope with it after returning home," she said. "It's a lot easier for family members to cope with a veteran's reactions when they understand why he or she is reacting the way they are, and that it's a result of their experiences in the war zone."

Andrea Carlile said at first she had no explanation for her husband's moodiness, withdrawal, depression, anger, nightmares, insomnia, and eventually substance abuse and violence. All are symptoms of traumatic stress.

"I didn't know what PTSD was," she said. "I just knew my husband was not himself at all."

Andrea said that counseling was the key for her and Wesley to be able to communicate with each other again and recover. She said their faith was also essential, but this was no overnight miracle.

"Anything worth having is worth fighting for; you've got to fight for it. That's our story," she said. "God gave us the strength to get through the steps, but you have to go through the steps."

Both she and Wesley have made changes.

"I have a lot more compassion," she said. "He has a lot more understanding that he has an issue that he needed help with. Both of those things have to work together for it to work. The wife has to have compassion and be able to be more patient at times. The veteran has to be willing to say there's something wrong."

Andrea acknowledged their work isn't finished.

"It's not been perfect. It's never gonna be perfect," she said. "I don't think he'll ever be completely symptom-free. He still has nightmares. He still gets tense at times. It's just different, the way we cope."

Anne Freund had encouraging words for couples like Andrea and Wes.

"As long as there is some degree of healthiness in the family to work with, there is definitely healing to be had," she said.

Andrea Carlile sees a purpose in her experiences. "Because

we had such a healing, we want to share it," she said. "We want to see other good endings ... it's still ongoing, but we were able to come through it."

★ ★ ★

Invisible Wounds: Voices of Experience

May 2007–August 2009

Post-traumatic stress is an invisible wound of war, one that may forever change the lives of its sufferers and their loved ones. These injuries of heart and mind are the price of military duty for some service men and women. Very often, a toll is exacted from their marriages and families as well.

When the Spouse Calls blog went online at Stripes.com in May of 2007, its earliest and most faithful followers were spouses of veterans suffering from various types of combat stress.

Several years into the wars in Iraq and Afghanistan, the effects of post-traumatic stress were becoming evident in the military population. Not every military family was equipped to deal with it or even recognize the issue when it surfaced. Many soldiered on alone, thinking they were the only ones. Some scoured the Internet for information and discovered the Spouse Calls blog.

As the moderator, I often provided information about counseling and other resources. More often, those who visited the site found their best sources of comfort and encouragement in one another and in their shared experiences. Commenters were most often spouses and veterans of the current conflicts, but messages came in from those whose loved ones served in the Vietnam War and World War II as well.

These messages are part of an important and ongoing chapter of American military life. Many were simple cries for help.

"My husband was in the Army National Guard and served in Iraq," wrote J. "He ... has since been suffering from PTSD. He refuses to get any type of treatment or counseling. ... Just a couple of days ago, he told me that he wants to separate for a while and just be by himself. I feel like my world is crashing down. ..."

Reading their words, I learned there were no easy answers and sometimes no happy ending.

"My marriage is over, and my ex-husband is no longer the same since he's been back from Iraq," wrote D.

"I miss the man I fell in love with," wrote K. "He can get angry for no reason, and he will lash out at me verbally. He knows he has changed, and he is not happy with it."

Changes in behavior and personality are common indicators of post-traumatic stress, and those who experienced this grieve as they would for any loss.

"He used to be a sweet, calm, funny guy that was always there for me. I used to tell him that hugging him was recharging my battery ... He has now turned into a judgmental, criticizing, angry person. ... I see so much hatred and anger in his eyes, the same eyes where I before saw laughter. ... That's my story. I am now left with letters, emails, and videos of a man who no longer exists."

Behaviors associated with PTSD affect families in very personal ways, making it difficult for them to reach out for help or share their pain. Those who had felt isolated by their situation were amazed to discover there were others suffering similarly.

"I really am not alone?" wondered T. "My husband has PTSD, and I really was feeling alone out here in the civilian world, thinking that no one out there understands and knows what I'm going through. Then I found this blog and site. Thank you, Jesus, I am not alone. ... Every story connects with what I have been or am going through right at this minute."

Others expressed similar relief.

"I can't believe there are so many of us out there living with the same kind of man," said L. "I thought for a second that it was me who wrote everything you did. Tears came rolling down my face when I read, 'He is a brilliant, fascinating, and unbelievably amazing man, but, I don't get much of that man anymore.' Even with four years worth of help, that hits home."

Both men and women reached out to find information and understanding. They asked questions, vented frustrations, and encouraged each other. A veteran, diagnosed with post-traumatic stress, expressed frustration with his own behavior.

"Trying to figure out what I'm doing to my wife ... I think I do all the things you guys say except cheat or hit my wife. I have finally gone to therapy, but I think I am a little late because I have been hurtful ... wanting a divorce one day and wanting her the next. Not interested in anything, including my kids. ... I blame her when it is clearly me doing this. ... I know you don't have to help, but I need it, and I have a seven- and four-year old ... I don't want them to think this is normal. My father was so kind, and I'm doing a terrible job."

Another writer, the spouse of a veteran with PTSD, responded compassionately.

"Don't walk, run to them and seek the help that you deserve," S. wrote. "That will send a huge message to your wife about how sincere you are about making changes. ... Bless you for recognizing your need for help. That's a huge step in the right direction. Let us know how you and your marriage are doing. I've found real support right here from others who understand."

Sometimes these conversations formed the basis for Spouse Calls columns, allowing these voices to be heard by a larger audience. Sometimes the online conversations simply linked people with a common interest: surviving the devastation combat stress brings to families and relationships.

Those who received therapy and counseling—as individuals, couples, and families—reported some hard-won successes. Some of their situations were dire, but determination was a recurring theme. So were love and acceptance.

"Every day I walk in the door, and the first thing I do is hug him, kiss him, and tell him how much I love him," wrote A. "The power of a loved one's touch can change the world ... He attends group every week and actively listens and talks. He shares a lot with me, but I know and now realize that he will never share Iraq with me. I do not ask either. ... Most importantly, I forgive him ..."

Another echoed the need for forgiveness.

"I am a strong woman. As an Army wife, I have learned that

sometimes I need to only be strong when he cannot be, to admit fault when it's mine, not to boast in his faults, to let the small things go, and above all, forgive. ... The life of an Army wife is different than that of a civilian wife. Then when you add war into the mixture, it changes the rules even more."

Learning the facts about treatment dispelled some of the fear and despair for more than one family.

"I did some research on my own on how to cope and help him at the same time. It made a big difference. It is less painful now that I can understand his behavior better. He is very loving and supportive of me. I let him be alone if he needs to ... He, too, understands the difficulties I have with him. ... I will continue to love him and be there for him no matter how long it takes."

Shared strength was another benefit of the conversations I read on the Spouse Calls blog.

"We are normal women put in very not normal circumstances. ... Maybe compassion is what it is about, compassion for ourselves. Maybe we just have to open to the idea of allowing ourselves to move toward health and peace and to know that our relationships are not failing because of us, or even our husbands. It is that third partner in there—Vietnam or Iraq—that tips the balance."

Sometimes it was hard to hear about these painful experiences, but important to know the very personal cost of war—to the troops who fight it and to the families who love them. At the same time, it was heartening to see the determination of these military families to survive, in spite of these invisible wounds, and to lift up one another in the process.

"Thanks so much for being out there, all of you. You make a difference on this endless tour," wrote E. to her fellow commenters.

W. responded, "It's early morning here, and I'm drinking my first cup of coffee, so I guess we are having a cup together ... Let's lift our coffee to the hope of another good day."

~

When Stars and Stripes *updated its online platform in the summer of 2009 to improve security and other issues, the new commenting format was no longer conducive to ongoing conversations between commenters. Additionally, past conversations are no longer available to read online. During the two years this forum was available, hundreds of comments were posted on the website by men and women affected by PTSD. This story contains snapshot of the challenges facing these military families.*

For active duty members and their families affected by post-traumatic stress, help and treatment is available through military healthcare. Veterans can find help through the Department of Veteran's Affairs. More information is available at the VA's National Center for PTSD at www.PTSD.va.gov.

★ ★ ★

Leaving Messages:
Meaningful Days

New Year, Old Friends:
Not the Same Auld Lang Syne

January 14, 2013

Our family received an extra gift in time to welcome the New Year, one that gave us more than we expected. It came, like Christmas in Whoville, without ribbons, tags, boxes or bags—unless you count the luggage. There was a fair amount of that.

All three of our children were with us for Christmas, a gift we no longer take for granted. Then, after Christmas, we were reunited with two families from a previous assignment—and all their children.

These families were assigned with us at Ramstein Air Base, Germany, just a few years ago. In those days, we gathered often with several other families for Sunday lunch after chapel services, for cross country meets and football games, for birthdays, graduations, or for no particular reason except that we enjoyed being together. We celebrated holidays and helped one another through deployment, illness, and loss.

By military fiat, two of our families are now stationed together in Virginia. By invitation, another family came here to visit, and by some miracle, every one of our combined eight children came, too. The "children" range in age from sixteen to thirty, and traveled from Texas, Colorado, California, and Slovenia to be here, so it was no small miracle that brought us all together.

In the days leading up to the visit, I wondered how all the kids would react to being together again. In young lives, even a few years make a big difference. They've each gone in different directions, to different schools, careers, states, and countries. Would they take up where they left off, or would they feel uncomfortable and strange?

I needn't have worried. Their divergent lives converged once again over movies, meals, and games. They exchanged old stories and the latest news from mutual friends, past and present.

They compared notes about college roommates, friends, and classes. They rediscovered similar tastes in art and music.

I overheard part of a conversation between two of the kids one day. They were sharing their common experience of coming home from college to a place that's never really been "home," except that their parents live there. All the familiar furniture and holiday decorations are assembled in a house that's home and yet it's not.

"So, you know what it's like," my daughter said to her friend, and I heard relief in her voice. There's comfort in being with someone who knows what it's like, who needs no explanation of the nuances, the lingering effects of living a transitory life.

When it's time to move or to say goodbye to friends who are moving, we military families usually have an instinct about those we will see again, the friends we'll stop and see when driving cross-country, the ones we'll drive across the country to see. In military life, our deepest friendships don't depend solely on geography, and they don't end with proximity. When we make friends for life, they remain a part of our family's story as surely as if they still lived around the corner.

Good friends are forever. Goodbyes are not. Old acquaintance might not be forgotten, but some experiences can't be recreated. What we truly relinquish with each move is a sense of place, the combination of friends and location we'll likely never experience again. We may be stationed with the same families occasionally. We might return to an assignment and even meet familiar faces there, but when a chapter ends, its pages can't be turned back.

In this time with our friends, though, we came close. Plenty of planning went into the event, but the atmosphere was serendipitous. There was an unexpected element—one we couldn't orchestrate—of auld lang syne.

We had a birthday party, went shopping, sat by the fire, did some sightseeing, watched a little football. Everyone ate and talked and laughed—a lot. The girls went for manis and pedis. The dads explored a local bike trail. The boys preferred skateboards and video games. One night, we went out for German food. Then we rang in the New Year with old friends and new ones. It was a microcosm of our friendship, compressed into less than a week of celebrating.

During those days, we were treated to shining glimpses of happy memories, yet we weren't reliving the glory days. We were making new memories, realizing our past relationships could also bear fruit in the present.

"It was nice to be with people we know," said my daughter, the day after everyone left. We know a lot of people, but I knew exactly what she meant.

This was the truest gift of the time we spent together: to be with those who not only know us, but who have known us. They are part of our family's history, our ongoing story. These are gifts that go beyond the same auld lang syne.

★ ★ ★

Fourteen Bucks and a Dozen Roses

February 8, 2011

The sign said, "One Dozen Roses—Only $6 for Valentine's Day Delivery." What was an eleven-year-old to think?

He figured he had more than enough.

Quite a few bills and coins rustled and rattled in the jar he used for his savings, left over from cash sent by grandparents for his birthday and Christmas. He knew he had way more than six dollars.

He probably spread the money out on his bed, counting it carefully before putting it all in his jeans pocket.

It's likely his mom thought he was off to play with the neighborhood boys when he hopped on his bike and headed down the street.

The flower shop wasn't too far away. He didn't even have to cross a big street to get there. He only had to follow the residential streets for a couple of blocks, then cut across on the dirt road that came up behind the shopping center.

His mom sometimes let him go that far anyway, he reasoned, to skateboard in the parking lot or buy candy and a Coke at the convenience store. Maybe she wouldn't mind—if she found out.

He parked his bike and went inside.

The lady behind the counter took his order for a dozen roses, and he gave her the address for the delivery. Good thing he remembered it.

But when she told him the price, he was stunned. It was almost ten times what he expected.

"The sign says it's only six dollars," he said.

The lady smiled—possibly trying not to laugh—and explained to him that was only the delivery charge.

"Well, this is all I have," he said, fishing in his pocket and piling the collection of bills and change on the counter. It added up to just over fourteen dollars.

She looked at the money and then at his serious, freckled

face. The blue eyes behind his wire-rimmed glasses might have been a little shiny.

"Who are these roses for?" she asked.

"My mom," he said. Maybe he thought about it, but he didn't tell the lady that he wanted to be sure his mom got flowers on Valentine's Day, even though his dad was deployed to somewhere he wasn't allowed to talk about.

"Well, I think that's enough to buy a dozen roses today," she said.

Perhaps her eyes got a little bright, too, when a smile of relief sneaked across his face. He thanked her, paid, and signed the card. Then he got on his bike and rode back home.

On Valentine's Day, when the vase full of big red blooms arrived, he had to reveal some of the story to his astounded and delighted mother, who asked, "How?" and "When?" and then "How much?" between hugs, kisses, laughter, and even a few tears.

Later, a dozen more roses arrived, ordered long distance by his father. Lucky woman—apparently the thoughtful apple doesn't fall far from the tree.

By the time the week was over, his mom had retold the story to everyone she knew and some she didn't.

I tried to interview those who saw it firsthand, but they were somewhat reticent. The boy, embarrassed by all the attention, wasn't eager to repeat it then. Now in college, he says some of the details are a little fuzzy for him.

So some of this story is guesswork. I was not in the flower shop that day in 2002. A few weeks after the memorable delivery, I visited the shop to find out who sold my sweet son a dozen roses, including delivery, for fourteen dollars and change.

But no one knew—or was telling.

★ ★ ★

Cross Purposes

April 3, 2012

The cross sat on top of a cabinet in the basement between a dusty autographed basketball and a framed crayon drawing. Why I put it there, I don't know. We have a collection upstairs, but this one was relegated to a room where we have exercise equipment, a second-hand sleeper sofa, and the third-best TV in the house.

The crosses displayed in our living room are decorative. One is Polish pottery in shades of blue and yellow. Another is polished olive wood. Others look like carved wood but are really plastic, more or less. A metal one was forged by my uncle, a blacksmith. Two are made of woven palm fronds from a long ago Palm Sunday service at a base chapel.

The cross in our basement is wooden and unfinished. It is rough and imperfectly attached to its base by a loose screw. Maybe that's part of the reason I put it downstairs. It's wobbly. Also, it doesn't match my living room decor.

The nondescript cross lay directly in my line of vision, while I was logging a couple of miles on the elliptical one day. I thought about the journey it had taken to arrive in the bottom floor of our home. It has traveled across an ocean or two, has been sometimes displayed and sometimes left to languish in a cardboard box.

My husband brought the cross home from a deployment to what was called an "undisclosed location" about ten years ago. The cross had been used for Christian chapel services in the field, then presented to him. The bottom is inscribed, "Operation Enduring Freedom," my husband's name, and the name of a unit with which he served.

Some may think a cross does not belong in a conversation about military life, or even in a living room. Many people are offended by crosses for good reason. In the first century, the Romans used them as instruments of defeat, torture, and criminal execution. Since then, crosses have been and still are used for many purposes and in the name of many causes that are far from sacred.

Regardless of those abuses, for Christians like me, the cross is not a symbol of death, defeat, or domination of one group over another. Essentially, it stands for one life given on behalf of others.

To be an honorable member of the US military, of course, one need not believe in this or any religious symbol. Regardless of belief or background though, military families do understand sacrifice.

With or without Christian imagery, rows of solemn grave markers in American military cemeteries from Arlington to Normandy, from Manila to Flanders Field, stand for lives given to gain life and freedom for someone else.

During the deployment in which my husband was given the wooden cross, he served with Air Force pararescue jumpers, who regularly offered their lives in exchange for the lives of others.

Their creed, embodied in its final four words, says this: "It is my duty as a pararescueman to save life and to aid the injured. I will be prepared at all times to perform my assigned duties quickly and efficiently, placing these duties before personal desire and comforts. These things I do, that others may live."

This is a statement of purpose, not of faith, yet it comes closer to what Christians celebrate at Easter than some sermons. It certainly hits the mark better than any politically charged assertions of faith emanating from the current campaign trail.

So I moved my husband's cross to the living room. It still needs a spot of glue to help it stand up straight, and it still doesn't match my furniture. Perhaps the reverse principle should apply. I would do well to remember its standard of selflessness, exemplified by my husband and all those who serve.

An ancient teaching, translated into English, says: "Greater love has no one than this: to lay down one's life for one's friends." Those who choose military service did not write this credo, but they live it.

★ ★ ★

Cherry Blossom Time

April 10, 2012

Four large men in full Bavarian regalia, alpine hats and all, were speaking German. At first, I thought nothing of it. It took me a couple of seconds to reach the Dorothy-esque conclusion, "Oh, I'm not in Germany anymore."

In fact, I was in Washington, DC, for an experience that comes from yet another part of the world. The German tourists and I were there to see the cherry blossoms.

Cherry blossom time in the nation's capital is an event that, like many other all-American things, didn't originate here. The trees that line the walkway around the Tidal Basin—home to memorials for US presidents and heroes—were a gift to Washington from the city of Tokyo one hundred years ago.

At the peak of their blushing glory, the blooms attract the city's locals, as well as tourists, foreign and domestic. I'm all of the above, I suppose. This is my first springtime since moving here from Germany, and I didn't want to miss the display.

In spite of the crowd, the mood was relaxed the day I went to Potomac Park. Jostling my way from the busy Metro through the equally populated National Mall, I heard snatches of conversation.

"What do the laws even mean anymore?" wondered a woman carrying a First Amendment picket sign.

"It's not a mall with shops," said a man to his teenage daughter. "It's where the monuments are. I think it was called a mall before there really were malls."

"Look at all the monuments!" said a mom to her preteen son.

"Look at all the porta-potties!" exclaimed the son.

It was a postcard day, with pink blossoms, dark branches, iconic white marble, and a flawless blue sky. The sidewalks and walking paths near Potomac Park were full of middle-schoolers on spring break, parents pushing strollers, walkers, runners, cyclists, and plenty of cameras.

In the cool grass under the trees, families spread blankets and picnic feasts. Baskets disgorged wine and cheese at one location, and peanut butter and jelly at another. Falling petals covered the ground and decorated hairstyles and hats of unsuspecting admirers.

When my children were small, we were stationed at Yokota Air Base, Japan, on the edge of Tokyo. Japanese friends introduced us to *hanami*, an outing especially for viewing blooming springtime trees, usually accompanied by a picnic.

Our Tokyo friends took a group of us American moms and children to a plum orchard on a spring day. Pink- and purple-hued trees and arched wooden bridges stood out like colorful embroidery against a silky gray sky.

We spread out plastic-lined blankets on the damp ground and removed our shoes to sit down. Everyone brought food to share, a Japanese/American picnic of sandwiches, *onigiri*, cookies, and bean paste sweets.

Like our friends in Japan introduced us to the flower picnic, *hanami*, the city of Tokyo has introduced these enjoyable pursuits to Washington.

After seeing the cherry trees, I traveled home via Metro. Even the conductor was in a springtime mood. His clear bass voice sang out, "Next stop Foggy Bottommm. Last stop in the District of Col-UM-biahh!"

I recalled the matter-of-fact recorded voice announcing, "*Nächster Halt, Vaihingen*" on the German S-Bahn and the soprano intonation of "*Roppongi, Roppongi*" on the Tokyo subway.

Here in my new home, it was comforting to find reminders of other places our family has called home. Too bad I didn't cross paths with the German quartet again. If they brought a picnic basket, I could sure go for *Brötchen mit Käse, bitte*.

★ ★ ★

Waiting for Spring

April 4, 2010

After three full months of snow and only one half-day's respite from school to show for it, our youngest son, Wesley, announced one morning that he was "done with snow." He philosophized, "If I don't get a snow day, then it's no good to me."

However, snow was not quite done with us. The ragged edge of winter dragged on, in dirty piles of leftover snow, gray skies, and muddy yards.

In early March, the remnants were almost gone when a new snowstorm brought six inches and another chapter of winter weather. The day of Wesley's pronouncement dawned on a marshmallow world, but he was disenchanted.

Snow should stay in December, January, and February where it belongs, he said. White Christmas is all well and good, but when the next holiday is St. Patrick's Day, a little green would be nice.

Even I grew tired of the monochromatic color scheme. I have always been a fan of winter, one of those annoying people who love snow, in spite of shoveling sidewalks, scraping windshields, driving on slushy roads, and withering comments from more practical individuals.

Perhaps it's an inherited trait, because my dad loved snow, too. His favorite duty station in his Air Force career was Eielson Air Force Base, Alaska, where snow is measured in feet, not inches.

Maybe my affinity for winter is rooted in grade-school memories of that assignment: neighborhood snow-shoveling parties and hot chocolate; sliding down mounds of piled-up snow; white Christmases; white Halloweens and Easters, too, for that matter.

But this long, hard winter has worn out its welcome all over the world, not just in my backyard. One February day, snow fell in every state except Hawaii. In my Oklahoma hometown, and many others, ice storms destroyed trees, damaged homes, and downed power lines.

My father died in the middle of this winter, when the snow he loved covered the ground here in Germany and his home in Oklahoma. Harsh weather and other circumstances dictated that his funeral would be put off until May. So I suppose that ever since this year began, when winter was at its deepest and coldest, I've been waiting for spring.

Am I waiting for a thaw, for a date on the calendar, for "Taps" and a folded flag, for closure, whatever that means? I don't know, but I could not just sit still and wait.

I went to Oklahoma in February. The ice was gone, the landscape gray and ravaged. The grass—usually brown in winter—was a colorless gray. Skeletal trees pointed broken, accusing fingers at the sky. Only ragged evergreens showed a subdued hue of something living.

It was not spring, but it was not a funeral trip either. It was a journey to reaffirm life, both new and enduring. I visited our son at college and tromped through a Texas snowstorm with him. I shopped and sipped coffee with my mom and sisters. I held my three-month-old niece for the first time. I had cake and ice cream with my grandmother at her ninetieth birthday party.

Life has an eternal spring—in new babies and nonagenarians—that spans every season.

I returned to Germany in time for the March snow and my son's denunciation of it. Well, springtime snow is nothing new here. One year, an Easter snowstorm blanketed the daffodils blooming in our yard. They survived to tell of spring. Their buried bulbs will rise to see many more.

As a wise man wrote, "... the rain and snow come down from heaven, and do not return to it without watering the earth and making it bud and flourish." (Isaiah 55:10 *NIV*)

I can wait for spring. I can take the snow—even without a snow day—because I know the daffodils are under there waiting, too.

★ ★ ★

Memorial Day

May 25, 2010

Blue sky overhead. Green leaves flutter in the Oklahoma breeze, and birds sing in the trees. Spring is here at last.

Newly turned red earth marks the place where one man will rejoin it. After traveling around the world, he returns to be buried surrounded by stones bearing familiar names. On this day, he is joined by family and friends in the town where he was born.

Blue uniforms. Six men in formation approach the place, carrying a polished wooden box and a flag.

The chaplain reads the words of an airman/poet over an airman who was never a poet, but who loved to fly and would have added his "Amen" to the words:

"High Flight" by John Gillespie Magee

Oh, I have slipped the surly bonds of earth
And danced the skies on laughter-silvered wings;
Sunward I've climbed, and joined the tumbling mirth
Of sun-split clouds—and done a hundred things
You have not dreamed of—wheeled and soared and swung
High in the sunlit silence. Hov'ring there,
I've chased the shouting wind along, and flung
My eager craft through footless halls of air.
Up, up the long, delirious, burning blue
I've topped the windswept heights with easy grace
Where never lark, or even eagle flew.
And, while with silent, lifting mind I've trod
The high untrespassed sanctity of space
Put out my hand, and touched the face of God.

Family and friends reach out for a nearby hand, holding back sobs. They watch with pride, heads lifted high, refusing to be overcome with grief or miss one moment of the honor due their loved one. It is a ceremony he would be proud to see, and they silently hope he does see it from the burning blue, the sanctity of space he now shares with God.

His remains will rest here in this small town cemetery, but not his soul nor his memory.

The honor guard folds the flag in silence, broken only by muted commands and the trill of a bird. One airman approaches the family and looks directly into the eyes of the widow.

"On behalf of the President of the United States, please accept this flag as a symbol of your loved one's honored and faithful service to this country."

Three times the rifles sound, and then the bugle plays "Taps." Day is done in the middle of a sunny afternoon.

Day is done for one veteran. One among millions who have served, lived, and died. Each is loved, mourned, and missed—during the funeral and for long afterward.

The ceremony is repeated often and sometimes too early for soldiers, sailors, airmen, and Marines. Some die in service and some live to retire, but they all surrender their lives for love of country and belief in the flag that will eventually be extended over their caskets and offered to their next of kin.

I live on the homefront. I've never experienced danger in the air or on a field of battle. But I've been on the front lines at the graveside of one who did.

On Memorial Day, how will you remember those who have lived and died in service to our country? Hit a few sales, enjoy a good book, gather with friends? By all means celebrate, make potato salad, burn a burger. Wave a flag. When you do, remember those for whom it has been spread and folded one final time.

★ ★ ★

The Star Spangled Banner

June 14, 2013

The evening event was studded with stars. Most were twinkling overhead, but quite a few were shining on epaulets among the attendees. Diamonds glittered as well, on rings, tiepins, and brooches.

Music was provided in the open air by "The President's Own," the United States Marine Band. The American flag entered with fanfare to the tune of George M. Cohen's "You're a Grand Old Flag," as the color guard marched across the green grass. When the phalanx reached the center of the parade ground, there was a brief silence before the band began to play the national anthem.

Civilian hands went to hearts. Those in uniform were already at attention, thumbs to seams, eyes on the flag. It was not long past the twilight's last gleaming, when the opening bars rose into the air, overpowering the background noises of local traffic and a few cicadas. Familiar notes lauded a familiar sight, the Star Spangled Banner wafting in the breeze.

Amid the sound of brass, woodwind, and percussion, an awareness dawned on some of the listeners. A voice was singing softly and tunefully, blending so completely with the music that the words were not noticeable at first. No performer stood at a microphone. The voice was not part of the program, nor was it simply an ambitious audience member showing off an under-appreciated talent.

The voice was not boisterous or pretentious, but gentle, audible only to those standing within a few feet of the singer. Like a song on an old fashioned radio getting warmed up, the words became clearer as listening ears tuned in, just in time to hear, "... the rockets red glare, the bombs bursting in air ..."

A few heads turned slightly, subtly, as hearers tried to find the source without disrespecting the flag or disturbing the singer. When they located him, perhaps it came as a surprise that he was in uniform. Singing along with the national anthem is not the way uniformed troops are expected to honor the flag.

But no one was about to silence him—not even those wearing the stars, though he was wearing stripes. They had all seen him earlier in the evening, and they knew he had borne the battle. His sacrifice was apparent by the medals on his chest and the evidence that his uniform did not hide. He moved a little stiffly, but walked without assistance. At first glance, he could have been any squared away Marine, and he was, but the scars on his face told a deeper story.

It was his voice that sang, his scarred lips that moved on the words, "... gave proof through the night, that our flag was still there."

He sang the words, in a voice that was clear but quiet, a voice that made listeners wonder if they heard the words or imagined them. But they were real, as real as his sacrifice.

The national anthem is a song about a perilous fight, of rockets, even of bombs and of defensive ramparts. It's a song about battle, though most who sing it have never seen one. Maybe this Marine remembered a painful dawn after a dark night, a battle that embodied the words of the song. Who would deny him the privilege of singing about them? Who would deny his listeners the privilege of hearing a warrior sing about the battle, perhaps remembering friends he lost in it?

Some Americans may rave about recording artists who perform the national anthem at sporting events. Others may rant about the ones who forget the words. Whether they've properly memorized the song or not, few of those performers could understand its meaning like that Marine. It's the same for most Americans. We can only sing it because someone else has been willing to live it.

None of those voices could compete with one Marine singing, "Oh, say does that Star Spangled Banner yet wave ... o'er the land of the free and the home ... of the ... brave?"

Because of men and women like him, yes it does.

★ ★ ★

Absence Makes the Dad Grow Fonder

June 19, 2012

My husband has a favorite photo of our children. All three of our kids are in the front yard on a sunny spring day in Georgia, where we lived at the time. Each stands on a skateboard holding a colorful sign. Each sign has one word, and in sequence they say, "Happy – Father's – Day."

My husband says he likes the picture because it brings back good memories. But he wasn't there when I took it. It's a picture of what he missed in June of 2003. He was in Iraq, and the photo was our gift to him on a Father's Day he could not share with us.

Like most military families, we have plenty of photos like that, but when my husband calls this one a good memory, I bristle a little.

"How can it be a good memory when you weren't there?" I ask.

"If I had been there, it would have been just another nice day," he replied. "I might have taken it for granted."

That's one luxury a military dad doesn't have—taking for granted any Father's Day he spends with his children. The same goes for Christmas, Easter, birthdays, baseball games, recitals, and other milestones of parenthood.

"Do you ever think about what you've missed over the years? What you've sacrificed during deployments?" I probe, interviewing him, though he doesn't know it.

But he won't be drawn into self-pity. He's never been one for regrets, especially about what he accepts as the price of his life's work, his calling.

"No," he answers. "Everyone I serve with is in the same boat." He accepts it as part of his mission: sharing the sacrifices of those he serves alongside.

I know better than to take this as an indication that he is not devoted to me and to our children. I married a military man, and I learned his convictions a long time ago.

A few months after our wedding, an American military action overseas brought concerns about deeper involvement. The potential that my husband, then a reservist, might be called to active duty and sent into harm's way was naturally frightening to me.

"What if you get called up?" I remember asking him as we turned out the lights and got into bed one night, after watching the latest unsettling reports on the ten o'clock news.

"Then I'll have to go," he said. He kissed me goodnight and was soon asleep. I stayed awake for a while, contemplating his acquiescence. I admired then, and now, his ability to weigh the cost of his commitment, accept it, and not lose any sleep over it.

The first deployment, it turned out, came several years later. As we said goodbye, I held our infant son, swaddled in blankets against the January wind. I knew then that my husband's service would exact a price from me, too—and our children. I've found it comes with many rewards as well.

Recently, I overheard a military spouse complaining about being the one to bear the weight of family life while her husband is away. It is hard, but I know I'm the lucky one. When my husband is gone, I get to be there for the cross-country meets, choir concerts, even Father's Day. Being there is my calling.

When he is deployed, my military husband is doing what he loves. I know he is lonely for those he loves more, but he chooses, rather than brood about the special days he's missed, to fully enjoy the ones he spends at home.

It's a quirk of military life that the family member who tethers us to the military is the one most likely to be absent. Whether he is near or far, his influence still shapes us. His commitment to service and love for us have guided and shaped the military life we are glad to live.

This Father's Day, the guy who makes all that possible at our house will spend the day at home—possibly relaxing in his favorite chair. He doesn't take that for granted, and we shouldn't either.

★ ★ ★

Born on the Fourth

July 4, 2010

In the headline there was no name, just a number: "1,000th GI killed in Afghanistan." I skimmed the story: Name not yet released pending notification of next of kin.

Numeric milestones seem so arbitrary. What makes 1,000 more significant than 999? Mourning families don't care about the math.

My Aunt June's life seems as distant from battlefield casualties as possible. She emails me regularly from her home in the peaceful hill country of Texas.

Just after Memorial Day she wrote: "I thought you might find it interesting to go to the *Kerrville Daily Times* website today. Read the article about the death of our local hero, Jacob Leicht.

"Unfortunately, he is the one thousandth death in Afghanistan. His family is very good friends with friends of ours, and we all live in the same 'neck of the woods.' I met his mother about a year ago when Jacob's leg was still healing from a horrible injury that happened on his first tour over there. His mom stated he was determined to go back to fight for his country, which he did.

"This is sad news, but wanted to share it with you."

I am an Air Force wife, living on an Army post overseas, just a time zone or two from both wars. But my sweet Aunt June was one of many friends and neighbors taking meals to the grieving family of one Marine. She's connected to the conflict in a way that I'm not.

So are many American families, because the connection is not about geography, just as the significance is not in the math.

The significance is in the history of a young man who gave up an ROTC scholarship that he feared might keep him from the front lines. Instead, Jacob enlisted in the Marines and was severely injured in 2007, just weeks into his first tour in

Afghanistan. He spent more than two years recovering and returned to Afghanistan in early 2010.

Jacob's mother, Shirly Leicht, said Jacob had always wanted to be a Marine.

"He was my strong little child, so that was a thrill for me,"
she said. "He had taken all of that strong will and turned it toward a very focused goal. He was a tough Marine on the outside
but just with a tender heart. He was just a sweet young man."

The Leichts' hometown paper reported what Jacob's younger brother, Jesse, said at his brother's funeral: "I'll always look
up to him. I'll always let everything he's done motivate me, push
me even further." Jesse enlisted in the Marines just nine days
before Jacob died in Helmand province. Jesse may never know
if his brother got the news in time.

Jacob's older brother, Jonathan, told a local reporter that
all the media questions about why Jacob would return to the
war after being wounded made him realize that "A lot of people
haven't met a lot of Marines."

I suppose that's true. Sometimes Americans only get to
know Marines, soldiers, sailors, and airmen through the stories told at their funerals.

"I attended Jacob Leicht's funeral services last Saturday,"
wrote my aunt.

"I think most of Kerrville either attended or lined the streets
to show their respects ... Four of his Marine brothers spoke,
and I have never heard such humbling words. Then, two of his
own brothers gave eulogies that just made my heart ache even
more so for his family. Our paper has been full of his legacy
and honor ..."

Honor for Jacob, who was born on the Fourth of July. He
would have been twenty-five today.

"Jacob being the 1,000th doesn't make him any better than
999, but we see it as a platform for the glory of God," said Shirly
Leicht. "We don't want anyone forgotten. So many people are
making sacrifices."

I can never skip over the recurring stories in *Stars and Stripes* listing the latest combat-zone deaths: Andrew, Edwin, Philip, Alvaro. Names their parents selected from baby books or family trees not long ago.

Like Jacob, each one is a name, not a number.

★ ★ ★

Election Day, Veterans Day
November 13, 2012

Inside the temple that pays homage to Abraham Lincoln, in addition to the larger-than-life image of the man, are complete texts of his most famous speeches. I suppose he's the only American politician deserving of a memorial large enough, and whose greatest orations were short enough for this to be possible.

Lincoln's image is flanked by the Gettysburg Address and his second inaugural address. Both acknowledge the sacrifices of the US military. One refers to the necessity of caring for families bereft by war.

The Lincoln Memorial faces the dome of the Capitol across the expanse of the National Mall, which is replete with symbols of historical sacrifices of those in military service.

Every name on the Vietnam War Memorial recalls a veteran's sacrifice and a family's grief. Every gold star at the World War II Memorial represents a hundred of the same. Tucked away in the less imposing DC War Memorial are names of district citizens lost in World War I. Among the monuments to freedom that populate the mall are reminders of the price paid to secure it, not just for our own country, but for others as well.

At the Korean War Memorial, an inscription says: "Our nation honors her sons and daughters who answered the call to defend a country they never knew and a people they never met."

The wide front steps of the Lincoln Memorial provide a wide view of the mall and are usually buzzing with sightseers. Few take the time for a quiet walk around the back of the structure to look across the Potomac River toward Arlington House. The former home of Robert E. Lee, situated on the crest of a hill, is the highest point of what is now Arlington National Cemetery.

Laid to rest there are many who paid the price for our nation, for the decisions made by every president since Lincoln. Some paid by giving their lives for their country. Others paid by living lives of service to their country.

Last week we re-elected our president. Some Americans danced in the streets at midnight. Others cried into their coffee the next morning.

On election night, I followed the news and commentary on social media. Opinions were thrown around carelessly. Frustrations vented bluntly. Victory celebrated exultantly. Freedom of expression is a privilege Americans love to exercise, and so we should.

We heard plenty of expression in the long run up to this election. Words count, but actions count more, and now it's time for action. Time for leaders to make tough choices and tougher compromises. Time for citizens to accept hard truths. As Americans cling to our rights, we also must realize our responsibilities.

Pundits shake somber heads over our polarized country. They say we're divided. We're also balanced. If one side can't overrule the other, then both sides have to work together. This is the stuff kindergarteners know, but Congress seems to forget.

On Veteran's Day, we honor those who serve America and the president without regard to politics. Our nation's leadership should care for veterans on the same equal footing. This means supporting them and their families, of course, but more importantly, it means crossing party lines to do what's best for the nation our veterans offer their lives to preserve.

Try whining to Mr. Lincoln about the ideological war between red and blue states. He might point out that the war between the Blue and the Gray involved real bullets and real blood, as well as a moral chasm.

Lincoln's words on healing for this nation are carved in stone. On election night, a young Army wife posted them on Facebook. They are as applicable in the electronic age as they were at the presidential inauguration of 1865:

"With malice toward none; with charity for all; with firmness in the right, as God gives us to see the right, let us strive on to finish the work we are in; to bind up the nation's wounds;

to care for him who shall have borne the battle, and for his widow, and his orphan—to do all which may achieve and cherish a just, and a lasting peace, among ourselves, and with all nations."

★ ★ ★

Giving Thanks

November 25, 2007

I was cutting up onions, and I was crying, but it wasn't the onions that caused the tears. It was geography. On a tiny island ten thousand miles from home, I was preparing for Thanksgiving festivities for which I felt neither thankful nor festive.

We had just moved from an assignment near my hometown to Guam, where Thanksgiving coincides, not with falling leaves and crisp weather, but typhoon season.

A typhoon moved across the island on Monday of that holiday week, leaving base housing with only sporadic electricity. We had power for a while on Tuesday, but then it suddenly went off again.

Weeks before, my husband and I had invited about twenty other transplanted islanders for a Thanksgiving feast. Now, all I had was a bunch of diced celery and onions, and a very large, very raw turkey.

So on Tuesday afternoon, I stood in my kitchen and cried over the onions. I thought I could feel at home with my husband and children anywhere the Air Force sent us, but how could we enjoy Thanksgiving with 80-degree temperatures, 100 percent humidity, no air conditioning, and no food?

"I have learned whatsoever state I am in, therewith to be content," chirped the Sunday school teacher in my head, quoting the King James. She was no help.

"Guam isn't a state anyway—it's a territory," I grumbled.

Interrupting this schizophrenic pity party was a vision— possibly from God, who was tired of my whining. It was a vision of the chapel, a building with emergency power and a kitchen with two big, beautiful ovens.

I called the chapel. The whole neighborhood must have had the same vision, because a turkey-cooking schedule was underway and filling up fast. I was able to get our bird a two-hour tanning appointment on Wednesday afternoon, which meant it had to be refrigerated until the next day. Our tiny generator could boost the fridge during outages, but not the oven.

We had electricity for only a couple of hours at a time Tuesday and Wednesday, so each day I cooked as much of the rest of the feast as I could and prayed we would have electricity on Thursday.

Thanksgiving Day our house was full, and our prayers were answered. The power was scheduled to be on until 4 p.m.—what luxury!

Our overseas extended family dined on pumpkin pies baked Tuesday night, dressing prepared on Wednesday, side dishes contributed by everyone who came—and the turkey.

Turned out the turkey's oven appointment should have been a little longer. When we sliced it, we discovered the dark meat was still a bit too pink.

On most holidays, carving into a partially raw turkey with a houseful of guests waiting to be served would qualify as a disaster. That year, it was scarcely a bump in the road.

After spending the night in the fridge, the turkey had to be sliced and then microwaved anyway. We just waved it longer. Don't tell Martha Stewart—or my mother. The meat was a little tough, yes, but I was simply thankful that it was thoroughly cooked.

Thankful—I was thankful to have electricity; thankful the typhoon damage was minimal; thankful to have our friends around us; thankful to have a turkey that was no longer raw.

I was a long way from home, but I realized I was also a long way from true hardship. The very circumstances that seemed to make thankfulness impossible caused me, in the end, to give thanks even more for the simple blessings of Thanksgiving.

★　★　★

Large Legend, Small Gifts

December 28, 2008

It wasn't very deep and crisp and even, but snow did lie 'round about as we drove away from Prague, the birthplace of the legendary King Wenceslas. The landscape was frosted, but the car was warm. With my husband at the wheel, I had the luxury of dozing, while Christmas music played on the stereo.

I woke up, recognizing the tune trickling from the speakers as we drove through the whitened countryside.

"Therefore, Christian men be sure, wealth or rank possessing.
Ye who now will bless the poor, shall yourselves find blessing."

It was "Good King Wenceslas." Life in the military has its trials, but seeing lands of history and legend is a pretty good payback—no extra charge for serendipitous musical accompaniment. Two days earlier, we had walked along Wenceslas Square in Prague and stood under the towering statue of the man himself on his horse.

The last notes of the song faded away, and so did the remnants of snow, as we approached the border with Germany, our adopted home.

I remembered a wintry night at another assignment in a very different landscape. There was no snow in California, but that particular December evening was chilly, and the background music was familiar.

After having dinner at a restaurant in Long Beach, my husband and I ducked into a warm coffee shop, a respite from the cold walk back to our car.

We ordered my caramel latte and Mark's chai tea and found some comfy chairs to wait for our hot drinks. Soon the doors opened again, and a man came in on a gust of winter air.

He was ragged—in clothing and expression. He didn't go to

the counter to order but, like us, found a warm spot and a soft chair.

Mark and I spoke in low voices, our eyes wandering to his sad presence. Living in a large city, we'd become accustomed to seeing needy people and panhandlers, but this man's detachment distracted us. We wondered if he had come in to get warm or to ask for money. He seemed content just to sit.

Our drinks arrived in festive red cups. Christmas music played softly. People gathered at tables, talking and laughing. The man sat.

"What song is that?" my husband asked. It was jazz, and the melody was elusive.

I listened. "Good King Wenceslas," I said.

We talked for a minute about the story of the nobleman who hiked miles in a blizzard to take food and firewood to a poor man.

"Then there's something I need to do," Mark said. He got up and approached the ragged man.

"Can I buy you some coffee?" The man nodded. Mark ordered and paid, and we quickly left. Warming our hands around our own half-empty cups, we were half embarrassed to offer such a small drop of generosity in a season celebrating the ultimate gift.

Good King Wenceslas wasn't really a king, and his name wasn't really Wenceslas. He was a duke named Vaclav. It's even possible that the story in the song never happened, but historians do agree that Vaclav was good, so good that more than a thousand years after his death, he is remembered and honored in his homeland.

Maybe he did give a simple gift of food and warmth on the day after Christmas a millennium ago, or maybe it was the songwriter who gave the gift by propagating the legend. Maybe the gifts should have been bigger. Maybe none of that mattered much to a man with a hot cup of coffee on a cold night.

★ ★ ★

A Child Is Born

December 20, 2009

My sister was in the delivery room of an Oklahoma hospital, about to have her first baby, but I was worlds away at a memorial service in Germany.

The chapel was full. I sat next to my husband, who was in uniform, like so many others there who had lost a friend and colleague.

Our minds were filled with questions. Those who stood before us to speak—to honor a friend and his faith—admitted they could not answer all those questions. Instead, they reaffirmed what they did know: The faith of our friend was the center of his life. His life was much too short. God has not changed.

I listened to their words about love, grief, and elusive comfort, and I thought of my sister and the baby soon to come. A liturgical quote ran through my mind. How does it go? "In the midst of life we are in death." Or should it be the other way around?

That evening, we gathered with friends to eat, to talk, and to draw strength from each other. Then we said good night, each falling asleep saying prayers for a family changed forever.

Next morning, in the dark hours before dawn, email brought tidings of great joy. A child was born.

My new niece had arrived—eight pounds of brand new life. Another family changed forever.

A friend dies, and we grieve. We face his mortality and ours, reminded how little power we wield over each day's events.

A child is born, and we celebrate. We face immortality, and remember again the power that belongs in larger hands than ours.

That day we felt the sting of death, but in the darkness a baby was born—as our faith was born with a child on a dark night.

During the memorial service for our friend, great faith was expressed, but it was evident that even the strongest faith would not wipe out the pain and loss. Nor would it provide all the answers to our questions.

The deepest questions of life and death may not be answered between the advent of the former and the finality of the latter. But faith whispers to me that there is something beyond this painful uncertainty.

Faith insists that life is more than what happens between cradle and grave, that birth and death are not just biographical bookends or elements of a mindless cycle, equal and opposite and each canceling out the other.

Now it's Christmastime. Despite evidence to the contrary, cards, commercials, and sermons declare "Peace on earth."

Is this just a hollow phrase when war shapes the lives of military families, when our community bears the scars of PTSD and IEDs, when a friend is gone and a widow's loss is still a raw wound?

Some questions will remain unanswered. But faith will also remain and, with it, hope and love—an intangible yet invincible trinity.

No, peace has not stilled all conflict in our world, but "Peace on earth" is not an empty sentiment. It is a statement of hope arising from the promises of faith and the birth of a child.

Faith does not ignore facts. Life is short. Death is real. Those who love will also grieve. These truths are solid, carved on countless tombstones, but they don't hold the final words for me.

For that, I choose faith that makes me sure of what I hope for even when I cannot see it.

I choose faith, because a child is born.

★　★　★

Decorations for Christmas

December 22, 2011

The vice president took a trip to Iraq last month to mark the end of the war there, or at least the end of US involvement in whatever conflict remains. All US troops are supposed to be headed home from Iraq by the end of this month, a late Christmas present for a war-weary military community.

But peace proves elusive. US troop strength no longer needed in Iraq will likely be redirected toward Afghanistan or the Pacific, where concerns are rising about China with its booming economy and unknown military intentions.

Wars and rumors of wars abound. All swords have yet to be beaten into plowshares, as an ancient prophet predicted. The titular "Isaiah Wall" across from United Nations headquarters in New York bears an inscription of that prophecy. When the UN was created after WWII, many believed that international cooperation could replace armed conflict with peaceful negotiation. Nearly seven decades later, strife and swords remain. The world still waits for peace and plowshares.

While we wait, we hope. Political and military revolutions continue, but Earth's revolution around the sun brings Christmastime around again. We sing the songs, light the lights, celebrate the season. Life still offers reasons to be joyful. Peace is present in our world, even if it doesn't rule.

In the paper last week, a front-page story described the panic caused in a Middle East city by the buzz of armed military drones overhead. In the South Pacific, the sound of planes has a different meaning in early December. Every year since 1951, aircrews at Andersen Air Force Base, Guam, have flown over the remotest islands of the Northern Marianas, delivering toys, food, and supplies. One year, my husband helped push pallets out of the back of a C-130 over those islands. This year's "Christmas Drop" parachuted about 20,000 pounds of holiday cheer to tiny islands without runways.

Congress wrestles with an unwieldy budget, and military families wonder how they'll be affected by inevitable cutbacks. Meanwhile, the United Service Organization sends care packages to troops. Moving companies and lawn-care businesses help military families for free.

Protesters occupy Wall Street and other public spaces, protesting the dominance of big banks and unfair business practices. On the other hand, the richest man in the world lost his title this year because he donated $28 billion—a third of his wealth—to charity.

Sophisticated Grinches steal online shoppers' identities, but secret Santas drop valuable gold coins into red Salvation Army kettles in Texas and Florida. Traditional thieves still swipe the occasional package from a front porch, while friendly neighbors leave holiday goodies on unsuspecting doorsteps.

Peace on earth seems unlikely when US presidential candidates—in the same political party—compare each other to megalomaniac dictators. Still, we believe our democratic process will survive another election.

The television news carries pictures of the aftermath of a suicide bomb in Kabul. The radio plays Christmas carols and greetings from military families stationed in Japan.

On a freezing December day last year, my husband bought an olivewood crèche. The wood came from Bethlehem, said the Palestinian merchant, a Muslim who made a long pilgrimage to bring his wares to the Christmas market in Rothenburg, Germany. Not long ago, it would have been unimaginable for such disparate creeds and nations to converge in a simple ornament for a Christian holiday.

This week, I took the nativity scene out of its box and put it in our dining room, a reminder that, in the absence of peace on earth, there is still good will and a reason to hope.

I heard the bells on Christmas Day
Their old familiar carols play,
   And wild and sweet

The words repeat
Of peace on earth, good-will to men! ...

And in despair I bowed my head;
"There is no peace on earth," I said;
"For hate is strong, And mocks the song
Of peace on earth, good-will to men!"
Then pealed the bells more loud and deep:
"God is not dead nor doth He sleep;
The Wrong shall fail, The Right prevail,
With peace on earth, good-will to men."

—Written by the father of an injured soldier,
    Henry Wadsworth Longfellow, December 25, 1864

★ ★ ★

Afterword

It all started when I thought I was just making coffee. One of my volunteer jobs at Yokota Air Base, Japan, was running the chapel coffee bar after Saturday evening service. I handed lattes over the counter while my husband, Mark, talked with those who lingered for caffeine and a little conversation.

An editor for *Pacific Stars and Stripes*, based in Tokyo, came to the chapel with his wife and daughter.

"Mark tells me you're a writer," said the editor one night, after a conversation with my husband, who is my best public relations guy.

"When I have time," I said, gesturing in the general direction of our three children—then a toddler, kindergartner, and second grader—playing follow-the-leader around the chapel annex. He gave me his card and said I should get in touch.

In an earlier life, I had been a journalist, a newspaper reporter, and editor. When I became a military wife and a full-time mom, I willingly gave up those other jobs, but I didn't give up on writing.

Family life was full and fulfilling. I would squeeze in freelance jobs when time and opportunity collided. I wrote for spouse club newsletters, local papers and magazines, and a few larger publications.

If I had been tempted to forget about writing during those busy years, my husband wouldn't let me. He'd often come home from work and ask, "Did you write anything today?"

Looking with exasperation from the baby in the high chair to laundry piled on the sofa, to our half-baked dinner, I'd answer with another question, "Does the grocery list count?"

As our children grew, so did the time I could devote to writing. My resume also grew by small increments. We lived out our military family life through peacetime and war. Sometimes I wrote about it—often only in my journal—and sometimes I just survived it.

Our family endured deployments, moves, separations, and transitions. We depended on each other and our friends. We missed our extended family when we were far away. We learned a new way of life after the events of September 11, 2001, and the wars that followed. We lived with the fallout of war in big and small ways. In all these things, we were not unique. We were like practically everyone else we knew.

In 2006, we moved to Germany, our third overseas assignment. When school began that year, I put all three kids on the school bus in the morning and picked up *Stars and Stripes* from my doorstep.

I had written a story or two for the paper when we were in Japan. I grew up in the military and then married into it as well, so I've always been drawn to *Stripes*. The newspaper is part of the history of military life and continues to record it as it unfolds every day. An idea took shape: I wanted to write a column for *Stars and Stripes*.

Maybe that idea had been growing for a long time, because after eight years and four moves, I still had the card from the editor at the coffee bar. I looked him up and found he was still at *Stars and Stripes*, now in their Washington, DC, headquarters. I sent an email to see if he even remembered me and to ask about writing a column for military spouses.

He remembered me, but the job news wasn't hopeful. No opening for a columnist, but *Stripes* did accept freelance travel stories. He also kindly invited me to send my resume and samples of my work. I did all of the above.

In September, I made a list of professional goals. Near the top of the list was "I want to write a column for *Stars and Stripes*." I waited, I looked for story ideas, and I prayed.

I've always wanted whatever work I do to fulfill God's purpose for my life. Now, I had this crazy idea: I wanted to be a newspaper columnist. Asking God to let me do it didn't sound very spiritual, but knowing he could do anything, I prayed about it anyway.

Around Thanksgiving, I got an email from my editor friend at *Stripes*. The paper wanted to add an advice column for military spouses.

"Are you interested?" he asked.

Of course, I said, "Yes!" I prayed another prayer here, which was simply, "Thank you, thank you, thank you," and went to work.

Spouse Calls began weekly publication in April 2007. Within a few months, what began as a question and answer format evolved into a feature that covered military life in a variety of ways. I interviewed spouses about their careers, families, and experiences. Sometimes I wrote about my own. Readers sent in questions, suggestions, and complaints. With two wars going on alongside everyday family life, there was no shortage of topics, everything from tipping at the commissary to post traumatic stress.

Over the years, Spouse Calls has evolved even further. It has been shaped, as I have been, by the path of my military life, by my family's experiences in it, and by the friends we've made.

In some ways, Spouse Calls began long before I wrote the first word of the first column. My military life is the foundation: Comforting my children during deployment and adjusting after homecoming, living through typhoons and earthquakes, baking cookies for neighbors and packing lunches for my kids. These experiences and more formed the reservoir from which I've drawn ideas, empathy, and insight.

When I was meeting people at a new base and staying in touch with friends from past assignments, without realizing it, I was building what became the original mailing list of Spouse Calls readers and contributors. It was that circle of military friends who generously shared their ideas and questions for the very first columns.

Since then, I've written more than three hundred columns. This collection includes many of my favorites and those I think are most reflective of my military life. Through Spouse Calls, I've written about good experiences and bad ones. I've shared joy and frustration, facts and information, with readers. I've received friendship and so many nice letters in return.

And it all started when I was simply living my military life, taking care of my family, making coffee, and saying crazy prayers.

★ ★ ★

Resources

Department of Defense/Veterans Affairs Suicide Outreach:
Resources for Suicide Prevention
www.SuicideOutreach.org

Department of Veterans Affairs National Center for PTSD:
Providing resources and information about post-traumatic
stress disorder for veterans
www.PTSD.va.gov

Just Moved: A ministry to women in transition
www.JustMoved.org

Kristin Henderson: Author, journalist, military spouse, and
advocate
www.KristinHenderson.com

The Legacy Project: A national, all-volunteer initiative, led by
best-selling author Andrew Carroll, encouraging Americans
to seek out and preserve the personal correspondence of our
nation's veterans, active-duty troops, and their loved ones
www.WarLetters.com

National Suicide Prevention Lifeline: 1-800-273-TALK
www.SuicidePreventionLifeline.org

Specialized Training of Military Parents: Federally-funded
training and information center established to assist military
families who have children with special education or health
needs
www.StompProject.org

Stars and Stripes: The only daily newspaper for military members and families serving around the world
www.Stripes.com

Tragedy Assistance Program for Survivors: Made up of and providing services to, all those who have lost a loved one on active duty with the Armed Forces
www.TAPS.org

Well Spouse Association: Advocates for and addresses the needs of individuals caring for a chronically ill and/or disabled spouse/partner
www.WellSpouse.org

Bob Woodruff Foundation: Created to provide resources and support to injured service members, veterans, and their families
www.BobWoodruffFoundation.org

Acknowledgments

To my closest friends and my generous fellow writers, most of whom are military family members. Thank you for always encouraging me in my work and in our shared experiences. Friends are among the best benefits of military life.

To *Stars and Stripes* readers in military communities all over the world who have sent in questions, comments, and ideas that have broadened and enriched the content of Spouse Calls. Without you, I would just be talking to myself. Thanks for listening.

To Robb Grindstaff, who offered me my dream job, writing a newspaper column, and then encouraged me to turn some of those columns into this book. You started it all, and I'm grateful.

To my editors at *Stars and Stripes*: Brian Bowers, Tina Croley, Jolene Carpenter (alias E.G.), Kate Maisel, and Sean Moores. Thank you for welcoming me into the *Stripes* family with open hearts and inboxes—from across the ocean, across the country, or just across town. It's a privilege to work with you.

To Karen Pavlicin-Fragnito, Kelly Root, and Meagan Frank at Elva Resa Publishing, where miracles seem to happen every day. Thank you for making this one happen.

To my children, Will, Jessie, and Wesley, who allowed me to write about their experiences and helped me tell the story of our military life. Thanks for understanding when I said, "I have to finish a column today," or "Just let me write this la-a-a-st paragraph," and "When you have children, you'll know how much I love you!"

To my husband, Mark, who has always believed in me, and encouraged and subsidized my scribbling obsession. Thank you for your service to our country and our family, and for asking me to serve alongside you. Because of you, I never wish for any other life but the one we have. I love you.